Praise For *Adult Students*

"Reliable, succinct advice that can help adult students make appropriate choices about pursuing a college education."
—*Nancy Hutton, Harvard Divinity School Student*

"This book is chock-full of usef  ust-have for any adult learner considerin{ nystifies what may be some of the bigg ge-level studies. The biggest mistake ad le to go to college is their lack of preparation. With this book, they will have better information, knowledge, tools and strategies to be successful. Adult learners comprise almost 50 percent of all students enrolled in higher education. If you are considering joining their ranks, this book may be the best investment you can make in your future."
—*Dr. Lee Bash, Dean of Graduate & Professional Studies, Averett University*

"This book is a valuable tool for adults who are returning to college. It is a wonderful guide to the application and self-evaluation process that goes into making the decision to return and then following through on that decision. *Adult Students* gives prospective students the knowledge to apply with confidence and the confidence to do so with less anxiety."
—*Laurel Stachowicz, Smith College Student*

"*Adult Students* is an easy read that addresses most of the issues that nontraditional students face when considering the big decision of whether or not to return to college. Program administrators and student advisors can benefit from the book's content as much as prospective students."
—*Dr. Charles Curry, Director, Adult Degree Program, James Madison University*

"Down-to-earth, practical advice. Written in an easy-to-read manner and sprinkled throughout with bits of humor. None of the pretentious academia that leaves you even more confused than before."
—*Torah K. Bontrager, Columbia University Student*

"Had this book been released 10 years ago, I would have probably returned to school earlier. My biggest fear about going back to school was the red tape. I feared missing some detail that would hinder my ambitions or looking stupid during the application process. What I have learned, and what this book will tell you, is that once you set your mind to it, you just need the right resources to get there. This is the right resource."
— *Heather Neal, Smith College Student*

Acclaim for Other Books by Gen and Kelly Tanabe

"Upbeat, well-organized and engaging, this comprehensive tool is an exceptional investment for the college-bound."
—*Publishers Weekly*

"Helpful, well-organized guide, with copies of actual letters and essays and practical tips. A good resource for all students."
—*KLIATT*

"Upbeat tone and clear, practical advice."
—*Book News*

"What's even better than all the top-notch tips is that the book is written in a cool, conversational way."
—*College Bound Magazine*

"A 'must' for any prospective college student."
—*Midwest Book Review*

"The Tanabes literally wrote the book on the topic."
—*Bull & Bear Financial Report*

"The first book to feature the strategies and stories of real students."
—*New Jersey Spectator Leader*

Adult Students

A Painless Guide to Going Back to College

2nd Edition

Gen and Kelly Tanabe

Harvard graduates and award-winning authors of
501 Ways for Adult Students to Pay for College,
Get Free Cash for College and *Get into Any College*

Adult Students: A Painless Guide to Going Back to College (2nd Edition)
By Gen and Kelly Tanabe

Published by SuperCollege, LLC
3286 Oak Court
Belmont, CA 94002
650-618-2221
www.supercollege.com

Copyright © 2007 by SuperCollege, LLC
Previous edition © 2004

Credits: Cover design by TLC Graphics. Illustrations by Terry Smith (www.t-smith.org). Back cover photograph by Alvin Gee (www.alvingee.com). Research and editorial assistance by Elaina Loveland.

Trademarks: All brand names, product names and services used in this book are trademarks, registered trademarks or tradenames of their respective holders. SuperCollege is not associated with any college, university, product or vendor.

ISBN: 1-932662-21-9

ISBN13: 9781932662214

Manufactured in the United States of America
10 9 8 7 6 5 4 3 2 1

Gen Tanabe, Kelly Tanabe
    Adult Students: A Painless Guide to Going Back to College / Gen Tanabe and Kelly Tanabe. --2nd ed.
    p.   cm.
Includes index.
    ISBN 1932662219
    ISBN 9781932662214
    1. College Guides   2. Education and Guidance
    3. Reference   I. Title

CONTENTS AT A GLANCE

TABLE OF CONTENTS

Chapter 4: Create A Winning Application / 63

Chapter 5: Craft An Admission Resume / 73

Chapter 6: How To Write A Winning Admission Essay / 79

We would like to dedicate this book to all adults who have made the brave decision to invest in their education to improve themselves and their world.

Promote Yourself By Going Back To School

Promote Yourself By Going Back To School

If you've ever been passed over for a promotion that you deserved...

If you've ever imagined yourself in a new career...

If you've ever wanted to challenge yourself personally and academically...

Then going back to school may be the answer for you. Sure it may have been years since you've opened a textbook or crammed for an exam. You may have skipped the SAT. Or maybe you've never even set foot on a college campus. And on top of that, you don't know how you can balance your studies with work or family. Or, more importantly, balance the checkbook to pay for your education.

All of these factors are easy excuses for why you shouldn't go back to school. But there are so many more reasons why you should.

Completing your degree or getting an advanced degree can propel you forward in your career. If you're changing careers, an education is the key to unlocking new opportunities and getting a jump start on the career you wish you had. For many, finishing a degree is the fulfillment of a long-held personal goal. Adults from age 25 to 85 are proving that you are never too mature to learn. This is one reason why adult students now make up the fastest-growing population on college campuses. There are now more than 3 million students who are over the age of 35.

And if you haven't heard this already, going back to school also provides financial rewards. According to the most recent U.S. census, with a college degree you will earn an average of $1 million more than someone who doesn't graduate from college over the course of your lifetime. More than increasing your income, however, going back to school will help you gain a personal sense of satisfaction like no other. You will finish the degree that you've always wanted, advance to the next level of your career or follow your passions to a new career. These rewards are more valuable than the size of your paycheck, and they are all within reach.

How This Book Will Help

Once you've decided to go back to school, the real work begins. Will pursuing a certificate or degree help you the most? How do you choose the right program for you? How do you combine your academic background and work experience to compose a competitive application? What do colleges or graduate schools want you to write about in an admission essay? How will you be able to balance all of your responsibilities with school? And, perhaps most importantly, how do you foot the bill?

This book will help you tackle these questions and the rest of the things that you need to consider when heading back to school. From deciding which program will provide the best benefits to putting together an application that best markets you to finding funds that are aimed at adult students, this book covers it all.

In addition to strategies for going back to school, admission officers and adult program directors will answer your most frequently asked questions. These experts have worked with adult students for years and even decades and will describe what they are looking for in applicants, mistakes that adult students have made in the past and what resources you may not know about that can help you pay for your education.

You will also find the inspirational stories of other students like you who have successfully gone back to school. They will explain how they came to their decisions, what challenges they faced in doing so and what mistakes they've made that they would like for you to avoid.

This book begins with how to choose the program that meets your needs. In Chapter 2, there are questions that you should ask when considering a program and descriptions of the advantages and disadvantages of certificate programs, community college, extension programs, distance learning, part-time programs, undergraduate programs and graduate programs.

Chapters 3 and 4 explain how the admission process works, what admission officers are looking for in applicants and how to apply. You will see what kind of information you need to provide and how to best showcase your accomplishments on the application.

For a quick snapshot of your accomplishments, some colleges also request a resume. Even though you might have experience with resumes, writing one for a college is very different than writing one for a job. Chapter 5 shows you what you need to craft a strong admission resume.

In addition to using the information you provide on an application form or resume, many colleges also require essays. Admission officers view the essays as one of the most important pieces of the application because they allow them to get to know you beyond the dry scores and grades of the application. You have the opportunity to describe your goals, your most important contribution or your personal thoughts and ideas. Chapter 6 is a complete writing workshop to guide you through the essay-writing process from selecting a topic to putting the finishing touches on your masterpiece.

Often it helps to not just learn about the theory behind writing an essay but to read some examples that have actually worked. Chapter 7 provides dozens of examples of essays that students have written to share their motivations and experiences with colleges and graduate schools.

Besides the essay, the next best way for admission officers to get to know who you are is to meet you. Strategies for approaching the interview are discussed in Chapter 8. And while some colleges don't require formal interviews, many have informational sessions in which you can use these same interviewing techniques.

Colleges and graduate schools also sometimes want not only your own opinion about yourself but the opinions of others. You may need to ask former employers or professors to write letters of recommendation on your behalf. Chapter 9 helps you select who will write the strongest letters and put together the information that your recommenders will need to write about you.

Chapter 10 helps you get organized and maximize the credits you receive for any previous studies, work experience or life experience. Some colleges require a portfolio to demonstrate what you've learned on the job or while raising a family. You want to make sure that you get the most credit for what you've already done.

Chapter 11 is the chapter that you've been waiting for. Loans, grants, scholarships, employer help, tax savings and other ways to pay for your education are covered in this chapter.

On a personal level, Chapter 12 explains how you can balance your school and family life and offers some strategies for making the transition from parent and/or employee to student again.

Overall, you will find that our approach for this book is to show rather than tell. You will read numerous examples of applications, essays and interviews to show you what has worked. We also include as many firsthand experiences of adult students as possible. It is our hope that you will be inspired by others who have gone before you, taking some of the stress out of going back to school.

Should You Return To School?

That is the $64,000 question, figuratively and sometimes unfortunately literally. There are three questions that we want you to ask yourself:

- Where are you now?
- Where would you like to be?
- Will going back to school help you get there?

These questions may seem self-evident, but you'd be surprised how many students don't think through them when deciding whether to go back to school. Before making such a large commitment of time and money, it's important to understand your motivations.

What are your reasons for returning to school?

Poor reasons for returning to school are:

- To escape the boredom of your current job without knowing how additional education will lead to a different career.

- To please someone else such as a spouse, friend or boss who thinks that you should return to school.

- To solve all of your personal or financial problems.

On the other hand, great reasons for returning to school are:

- To advance your current career.

- To receive a raise or promotion.

- To change careers.

- To fill a necessary gap in your education.

- To achieve a personal sense of accomplishment.

If after carefully examining your motivations you determine that going back to school is the right decision, the real work begins. Read on.

TWO

How To Choose The Best Program For You

Finding A College That Fits

Have you ever walked into a snooty boutique only to be ignored by the even snootier staff? Have you ever found yourself at a party where you don't know any of the guests? If so, then you know how uncomfortable it is to feel out of place. Unfortunately, this can also happen when choosing a college or university. No two schools are the same, and while one may make you feel at home, the other may make you feel like you just landed on an alien planet.

The key to picking the right school is to take the time to do some self-reflection. Many prospective students skip this step and jump ahead to picking a college based on the school's glossy brochure or website. But before you even look at schools you need to take a long, hard look at yourself and ask some serious questions about what you want. Not only will this greatly improve your odds of ending up at a school that's right for you, but it will also come in handy when you need to express these feelings in your applications and admission essays.

So let's take the first step to picking the perfect college by uncovering what you really want.

What Do You Want?

When you were in high school you may have taken a career assessment test. This was the exam in which you used a number two pencil to bubble in page after page of questions about what you enjoy, your strengths and desires for the future. Then, depending on how long ago you went to school you either used the answers to sort through a bunch of index cards or simply waited a few days to receive the results by computer. In either case what you ended up with was a list of careers that supposedly fit your personality and talents. Based on your results, you were declared fit to become an accountant, attorney or even long-haul truck driver.

While these tests sometimes produced interesting answers, the idea behind them is sound. It's important to analyze your strengths, weaknesses and goals to figure out what you want out of college before you start applying to a bunch of schools. As you've grown older (and immensely wiser) you've probably realized that life is complicated and there are few cut and dry answers. Otherwise, we would all have followed the results of those career assessment tests, and some of us would be driving tractor-trailers instead of writing books.

Therefore, our test to help you find the right college is not multiple-choice. At the end of the test we won't give you the names of three perfect colleges. Life is just not that simple. However, we do promise that by taking our test you will discover what you are looking for in a college and what aspects of a school are important to you. With a clearer understanding of what you want, it will be much easier to pick a school that satisfies your needs. So sharpen that number two pencil and take our test to help you figure out what you want. And you thought you only have to take tests after you get into college!

The "What I Want" Test

Career goals:

- By going back to school, do you hope to advance in your current career or to change careers all together?

- If getting more education will help you advance your current career, what specific knowledge and/or degrees do you need to get the promotion you desire?

- If you are planning to enter a new career, what are your motivations for doing so, and how much education do you need to realistically get a job in this new field?

- How will going back to school help you achieve either of these career goals?

- For your career field, how much does the academic reputation of the college or university count?

■ What specific classes or subject areas must you take for your career objectives?

■ In order to achieve your career goals, is it necessary to receive a bachelor's or advanced degree, or do you just need to obtain certain skills or update your skills with a certificate program?

■ In talking to people already in your desired career, what recommendations do they have about the type of education required to be successful?

■ Is it important that your college be in an area where there are work opportunities such as internships related to your career?

■ Are you sure more education wil help you achieve your desired career goals?

■ Where do you see yourself in your career in five years? Ten years?

Academic goals:

■ What academic areas interest you?

■ What would you like to major in?

■ How sure are you about this major?

■ What if you end up hating this major? What would you study instead?

■ How will your major help you achieve your career or personal goals for returning to school?

■ In what kind of environment do you learn best? Small seminars? Large lectures? Interactive discussions? Lectures?

■ Do you have any previous college experience? Will you be finishing a degree that you started? Is it important that credits from previous courses can be transferred?

- How much interaction with other students and professors do you want?

- How well will you be able to work with students younger than you?

- Can you put in the necessary study time to be successful in-school? Do you have a place in your home that is conducive to studying?

- Is academic reputation important to you?

Balance:

- How much time do you have to dedicate to your studies? In other words, can you afford the time to be a full-time student? Consider not only the time that you will spend in classes but also time for commuting and studying.

- How will your class schedule fit with your other commitments such as family, work, socializing, etc.?

- Will you be able to spend the time that you need with your family if you attend a full-time, part-time, evening or distance learning program?

- Will you be able to find childcare if you need it?

- Are you willing to move to attend a school?

Money:

- Can you afford to quit your job to go to school, or do you need to hold a part-time or full-time job?

- Are you willing to make major financial sacrifices to pay for college? Is your family?

- How much money have you saved to pay for college?

- What tangible goods (i.e. new car, home improvement) will you have to postpone to pay for college?

- Are you willing to borrow money to pay for tuition? How much debt are you willing to incur?

Timing:

- Is now the best time to return to school?

- Since you'll be in school for anywhere from a few months to several years, what future commitments may conflict with your education?

Personal:

- Are you ready to be a student?

- Are you willing to do homework, take tests and attend lectures?

- Do you feel a burning desire to return to college? (If not, you might want to reassess whether you are truly ready to go back.)

- Do you have a support network of family and friends who can encourage you through your studies as well as assist you during busy times?

Put your pencils down. This is the end of the test. Not all of these questions can be easily answered, but by forcing yourself to think about these issues you should have a much clearer idea of why you want to return to school, what's important to you and what kind of program will match your goals. Now that you know what you want, let's take a look at some of your options.

Opportunities For Learning

Shopping for jeans has gotten a lot harder with the explosion of choices. It's not enough anymore to know your size and price range. You also need to know whether you want relaxed fit or slim fit, dark blue or faded, boot leg or flared. The possibilities seem endless (especially when a spouse is waiting outside of the dressing room door). But having choices allows you to select the perfect pair of jeans. It just takes a little more quality time in front of the dressing room mirror.

When it comes to selecting a college or graduate school, you'll find that you have a myriad of choices. Since you went through the exercise to determine your needs earlier in this chapter, you know what you want and can start to explore each of these options to find the right program for you.

The following is a quick overview of the most common choices. It is also helpful to learn the lingo of higher education. Many colleges offer programs that combine the following options:

Course Options

There are basically two types of college courses that you may take and each has its own advantages and disadvantages:

Noncredit courses. Many colleges allow adults to register for specific noncredit courses. These are courses that will not count toward a degree and are intended to provide skills and knowledge that will help you in your professional development. If you just want to acquire new skills or knowledge or are going back to school for personal enrichment, then noncredit courses are a low-stress way to do it. Plus, you often don't have to go through the complex process of being accepted into a degree program. Besides students who just want to take a few specific courses, noncredit courses are also an excellent way to acclimate back into being a student. So before you jump headfirst into a degree program you might want to take a few noncredit courses to make sure that you are ready for the academic rigors of college. You can also use noncredit courses as a refresher for basic skills that you might have forgotten (i.e., math) so that you'll be prepared for your degree program when you start.

Credit courses. These are courses that are part of an organized program to earn a degree or certificate. However, you may take credit courses even if you aren't seeking a degree. The difference between these courses and noncredit courses is that if you successfully pass the class you receive credit and can use that credit later on toward a degree. Be careful, however, about taking courses from a number of different schools because they may have different rules about which credits will transfer. Of course, to receive credit for a course you must also earn a passing grade. This makes credit courses a little more stressful than noncredit courses.

Degree And Certificate Programs

Many students who go back to college want to earn a degree. While individual schools may differ, you'll find that the most common programs you'll encounter will fall into one of the following categories:

Certificate program. Certificate programs are aimed at students who need to update their skills, acquire specific new skills, earn credentials or even change careers. They are usually shorter than degree programs, lasting for several weeks or months rather than years. If you take all of the classes in the series, you receive a certificate. One advantage of a certificate program is that you don't need to dedicate as much time or money to receive a certificate. For career advancement a certificate, which shows that you have learned a specific set of skills or body of knowledge, may be all you need. The disadvantage of a certificate program is that it is not as comprehensive or flexible as a degree. Obviously, if it takes four years of study to earn a bachelor's degree and only four months to earn a certificate, the bachelor's degree signifies a much greater amount of learning. One other advantage of a degree is that it is required to pursue an advanced degree. Most certificates will not allow you to advance into a graduate program.

Undergraduate degree program. Undergraduate degrees include associate's degrees from community or two-year colleges and bachelor's degrees from four-year colleges. You may receive your associate's degree from a two-year college and then complete the third and fourth year of your college education at a four-year college to receive a bachelor's degree. Earning a degree signifies that you have mastered a field of knowledge. When you hear the phrase a "college education," most people mean that you have earned an associate's or bachelor's degree.

Graduate program. If you've already obtained your bachelor's degree, you may further your education with a graduate degree, which is usually a master's or doctorate. There are also a variety of professional degrees such as Master's of Business Administration (MBA) and Jurist Doctorate (JD). Master's and professional programs typically require one to three years of study, and doctorate programs may require four to eight years. When it comes to education, this is the pinnacle.

Accelerated program. Some schools offer programs that allow you to obtain a degree in less time than is usually required. For example, if you have a number of college credits, you may be able to receive your bachelor's degree in about two years. An advantage of this type of program is that you will spend less time out of the workforce, but the big disadvantage is that because the program is accelerated, you will need to concentrate more time on your studies. There are accelerated programs for both undergraduate and graduate degrees.

Colleges And Universities

When it comes to where you will take courses and earn a degree or certificate, there are several choices:

Vocational or technical schools. These are specialized schools that teach skills that are directly transferable to a specific career. Automobile repair, medical assistance, cosmetology and computer networking are all examples of subjects taught at vocational schools. Vocational schools may award certificates, associate's degrees and even bachelor's and master's degrees. The main disadvantage of vocational schools is that they offer limited courses. This is not a problem if you are going back to school to learn a specific skill, but for students who have more general interests, a community college or university may be a better choice since it offers a much wider selection of classes. In addition, vocational or technical schools are often more expensive than other options such as community colleges.

Adult schools. These programs are typically run by state or county governments to provide specific skills to adults. They often offer practical courses such as computer training. Adult education is an a la carte system where you pick and choose the classes that you want. You usually receive a certificate of completion for these courses but not college credit.

Community college. These are the hidden gems of the education system. Cheap, local and with open admission policies (i.e., anyone will be accepted) they offer you the chance to attend school for two years or more to receive your associate's degree. Then, you may transfer to a four-year college to receive your bachelor's degree in another two years. Attending a community college may be a great option to help you ease back into studying, take basic requirement classes and save money. Community college is where many adults get their first taste of returning to school.

Four-year college or university. There are more than 3,500 colleges and universities in the U.S. offering private and public educations. The advantages of four-year colleges are the resources that they have and the size and breadth of the faculty. Four-year colleges are more competitive to gain admission into than community colleges and are often more expensive. However, you cannot beat a four-year college or university for the range of courses, degrees and learning opportunities.

Continuing education. Many four-year colleges and universities have established continuing education or extension programs just for adults. These are typically held in the evenings and are usually open enrollment, which means that you don't need to go through a selective admission process to get into the program. Best of all you can earn complete degrees and graduate certificates without having to become a full-time student. Most of the faculty is also the same that teach during the day at the college or university.

Distance learning. Distance learning programs offer the same type of certificates and degrees as traditional colleges. The big difference is that you take courses from the comfort of your home. Many are online only, where you have "discussions" with your professor and classmates on the Internet. Other programs combine online learning with in-person learning. An advantage of distance learning is flexibility. You don't need to commute to classes, and you can participate in class discussions and complete assignments on your own time. Disadvantages of distance learning are that you may not have the face-to-face interaction that you do in a regular classroom setting. Plus, it takes a huge amount of self-discipline to complete a distance-learning program.

Is Distance Learning For You?

Imagine sitting in the comfort of your living room in pajamas and slippers while participating in a classroom discussion of English literature. Seem impossible? Through distance learning, you can do exactly this. Distance learning provides courses over the Internet or through other electronic means, allowing you to learn without leaving your home or stepping on a college campus. It can provide the flexibility that you need to do schoolwork around your existing schedule.

However, while distance learning sounds attractive, it is not for everyone. Some students just don't learn as well when not in the presence of a professor and roomful of students. In fact, some students find that it is the classroom setting with the interactions, debate and discussions continued after class in hallways and student centers that is the real benefit of going to college. Plus, there's less guilt from skipping a distance learning class than in-person classes. This means that you must be extremely self-motivated to attend the online sessions and complete your assignments.

Yet, despite these drawbacks, distance learning is still a viable option for thousands of students. Here, we outline how distance learning programs work, how to figure out if they are right for you, how to select the best ones and how to succeed in a program.

How Distance Learning Works

As its name suggests, distance learning basically means that you will receive instruction from a distance, typically via the Internet. There are some distance learning programs that incorporate cd-roms that you use with your computer or lectures via remote television broadcasts. Through distance learning, you may take individual courses to learn specific skills or even complete an entire degree.

Typically, instead of going to a physical classroom, your meeting place is the Internet. Work is similar to that of regular courses. You will still have reading assignments, homework, quizzes and exams. What's different is you do not need to meet in a classroom at a specific time for discussions, and you can work independently. Professors give assignments online or via email, and students are often expected to participate in discussions through online message boards. You email assignments into your professor, and he or she grades them and provides feedback through email as well. Since you usually don't have to participate in the discussions at the same time as the other students, you can fit the course to your schedule—such as after 10 p.m. when your kids go to sleep. There are, however, still deadlines for when papers and assignments are due.

How To Tell If You Are A Distance Learner

To determine if distance learning is right for you, see how many times you answer "yes" to the following questions. The more often you do, the more likely it is that distance learning may work for you.

- Are you disciplined enough to complete your coursework including homework on your own schedule while still meeting the course's deadlines?

- Do you like to work independently with minimal in person interaction with others?

- Are you proficient at using a computer to visit websites, send email and participate in online discussion groups?

- Can you learn the material you want to study primarily through written instructions without much interaction from the professor?

- Will you be willing to dedicate as much time to your distance learning program as you would to a traditional classroom program?

- Does your schedule allow you to focus on your course-work every day?

- Will you be motivated enough to complete your program even if you never speak to another student or professor aside from email and message boards?

If you answered "yes" to most of the questions above, then you should consider the benefits of distance learning. One of the greatest benefits is the flexibility that it offers. Because you do not have to go to classes at a certain time, you can study when it's more convenient for you and you may not need to quit your job to fit your studies into your schedule. You will also save time by not having to commute to campus. This is especially helpful if you live in a remote area or if it is difficult for you to travel. In addition, you can take courses from institutions across the country. You are not limited to the courses offered by your local college or university.

Choosing A Distance Learning Program

Unlike choosing a traditional college or university program, you don't necessarily have to choose a distance learning program within driving distance. In fact, you can choose one out of town or out of state. However, there is more to choosing a program than simply pointing and clicking on the first one that you find. Here are some factors to consider:

Accreditation. Make sure that the program is fully accredited, especially if you plan to pursue a degree. Employers as well as other colleges and universities place a high value on programs that are fully accredited.

Certificate or degree. Some distance learning programs are aimed at providing you with a certificate while others allow you to earn a degree. Make sure that the program meets your academic goals.

Course selection. You'll want to make sure that there are enough courses offered to meet your needs and interests. You can do this by looking at the course catalog. Also, investigate how large the classes are to determine how much attention you will receive as a student.

Format. There are distance-learning courses that are entirely online and those that require periodic meetings on campus. Some students combine distance-learning courses with on-campus courses. Some follow the same schedule and pace as traditional quarters and semesters while others are accelerated, which means that you cover a larger amount of material in a shorter amount of time. Distance learning programs offer a variety of formats, meaning that you will need to choose the one that works best for you.

Support. Investigate how much support is offered for distance learners. How much will you be able to interact with your professor? Is there support for technical problems? Will you have access to the same resources and facilities as on-campus students?

How To Succeed With Distance Learning

Some students have difficulties with distance learning because of the technology or the lack of face time with professors and classmates, but there are steps that you can take to help you succeed.

Get familiar with the technology first. Before signing up for a distance-learning program, get friendly with your computer and the Internet. If you need to, take a course at your local community college or adult learning center or have someone tutor you. This means that you will have one less thing to worry about when you are taking the class.

Start small. If you are hesitant about distance learning, start with one class rather than jumping in and taking a number of courses. This will allow you to get your feet wet before making a huge commitment to multiple classes.

Make the most of your classmates. Just like you, your classmates are there to learn. Don't be afraid to rely on them for help. Use email to stay in touch and have discussions with your classmates. Similar to if you had taken a course in a traditional classroom setting, you'll learn a lot from your peers.

Use the resources available to you. Communicate with your professor if you have questions or problems. Your professor will want to know if you are struggling with the material or if you need extra help. In addition, your school may offer extra tutoring help or other resources.

How To Narrow Your Choices

Once you have decided which type of classes or program you would like to attend, the next step is to narrow your choices. This is where your research skills come in handy. It's important to do a little investigative reporting about the schools to make sure that you find the one that best fits you. Fortunately, you can learn a lot even if you don't have a lot of time. Here are some of the best ways to research a school:

College directories. There are numerous directory books and online guides that give you descriptions of the colleges and universities. Check a book out from the library, or look at an online directory like the one at www.petersons.com.

Websites and brochures. You can get a lot of information directly from the school itself. Many colleges and universities have extensive information about their programs on their websites, where you can also look at the course catalogs and request more information by mail.

Visiting. Nothing tells you better whether a school is a fit than visiting the campus. Sit in on a class, observe student interactions and ask questions of current students to get a true feel for what it's like to be a student there.

Informational sessions. Many admission offices host nights where you can learn more about their programs either on campus or at community centers. This is a great way to learn a lot in an hour or two. Take the time to speak individually with a representative before or after the session. This may be the person who will review your application so it doesn't hurt to leave a good impression. Be sure you have a list of questions to ask.

Admission office. If you aren't able to make it to an information session, consider the admission officers as goodwill ambassadors of the college or university. They will answer all of your questions about the program. You can call or email them directly.

Financial aid office. Contact the financial aid office to find out about any special loans, grants or scholarships that you may be eligible for as an adult student. Some schools have scholarships that are specifically aimed at adult students.

Adult education office. Since your needs as an adult student are different than those of traditional students, some schools have offices that are specifically dedicated to you. This office will help you learn about special programs and services for adult students and may help you with the application process.

Current students and recent alumni. One of the best ways to research a school is to learn from those who are there now or who were recently there. Ask lots of questions about the program from current students or alums.

Besides these typical places to find out more about a school, use these less well-known resources to get the real scoop on student life:

Student publications. Because these are aimed at current students rather than prospective students, you'll get the real story about what's happening on campus, what issues are hot topics and the strengths and weaknesses of the school. Many school publications are available online through links on the school's website.

Bulletin boards. By reading what flyers are up on the bulletin boards or kiosks, you can get a sense of the student activities, speakers who are visiting and research opportunities.

Individual student websites. Another way to get the students' perspectives is from their websites. Many colleges have links to individual students' websites where you can learn about how they really feel about their school.

Campus organization websites. Get information on campus organizations directly from the organizations themselves to see how active they are, what events they have and how you can get involved.

Department of your major. If you contact the department of your potential major, you may be able to speak with a current student or a department administrator. Ask about courses that interest you, research opportunities and what students in the major do after graduating.

Professors. Even though they are busy teaching, many professors like to take time outside of classes to help future potential students. You can get their telephone number or email address from the department. Ask about the classes that they teach and research that they are doing.

Switch From Researcher To Analyst

Just like when you took the self-assessment test and interrogated yourself about what you want from a college, you need to grill each college you are considering to uncover how well it matches your needs. As you are researching the colleges or universities, keep these questions in mind:

Academics

■ How strong is the school in your field?

- What is the reputation of the college?

- Are there professors who are researching subjects that are of interest to you?

- How accessible are the professors?

- How many other students are currently in your major?

- How large are the classes?

- What are the requirements to earn a degree? How many classes do you need to take? Do you have to write a thesis or do a final project?

- Are classes taught by professors or teaching assistants?

- What kind of research opportunities will you have?

- Does the school provide remedial classes in case you need to refresh your knowledge?

- Is low-cost tutoring available?

- Is going to school part-time or during evenings and weekends an option?

Career preparation

- What services does the career services office provide?

- Will the school help you find a job after you graduate?

- Does the school have a strong alumni network?

- Are summer internships available at nearby businesses?

- What companies recruit on campus, and what positions do they recruit for?

- Will the program provide you with the skills or education that you need to reach your career goals?

Special considerations for adult students

- Does the school have an adult services or adult education office?

- Does it provide childcare?

- Are the classes held at a time when you can attend?

- Are the university offices, libraries and student centers open when you will be on campus?

- Does the college understand the special needs of adult students?

- How many other adult students are enrolled?

Social

- Are there activities and organizations in which you can get involved?

- Is there an organization for adult students?

- What kind of networking opportunities are there for adult students?

- Do you feel comfortable on campus?

Financial aid

- How much does the school cost?

- How well does the school meet the financial need of its students?

- Does the school provide loans, scholarships or grants for adult students?

- How helpful are the people in the financial aid office?

Practical considerations

- How far is the school from where you live?

- Can you attend the school part-time?

- Does the school offer weekend, evening, distance learning or accelerated programs?

Creating A Short List

Now that you have discovered what you want from a college and have researched each of the schools that you are considering, you can make a short list of the three to five schools that you are most interested in attending. It's time to request applications and start applying. If you are applying to more than one school, you'll probably wait until you get your acceptance letters and financial aid offers before you make your final decision.

Picking the right college is not easy. You need to be honest with yourself about why you are going back to school and what you need to be successful. You also need to research each of the colleges to make sure that they offer programs that fit your schedule and won't make you feel out of place. While it might seem like a daunting task in the beginning, if you spend the time to take all of these steps before choosing a program, you will end up with the best match possible.

Frequently Asked Questions

About Going Back To School

Frequently Asked Questions

In this chapter we have assembled a group of crack admission officers for a frank conversation on what adult students need to consider when applying for admission. Over the years, these professionals have seen it all.

Q. Why do adults go back to school? Are there any reasons why it would not be a good idea for someone to return to school?

Dr. Lee Bash
Dean of the Division of Lifelong Learning, Baldwin-Wallace College

Adults typically cite career issues as their primary reason for returning to school. However, I've noticed another phenomenon that happens so frequently that I'm convinced there is often another, deeper reason for going back to school. Adult learners initially give pragmatic reasons for enrolling saying, "I need this piece of paper so I can get a promotion" or "a new career." But after the student becomes immersed in her studies, she often tells us, with animated enthusiasm, how much she loves being a student. Often these students don't stop even after they complete their program. Many will go on to finish a degree or even additional degrees. It seems that for these students at some point in their lives they had this epiphany that led them back to school. It may not happen all at once. In fact, the idea to return can take many years to develop. But when these students do enroll, it is already with a strong sense of purpose.

On the other hand, when students come to us citing external motivators like a boss, loved one or parent as the reason they are seeking admission, they are much less likely to complete their studies. In fact, according to our statistics almost 50 percent of all adults are unable to achieve their objective—due in large part to how daunting a task it is. It's important that students don't rush into these decisions and take time to do some serious introspection. If there isn't a "fire in the belly" for retuning to school then the odds are the student won't be able to overcome the many challenges.

Q. What factors should adults consider when deciding whether or not to go back to school?

Janet Pelto

Lifework Consultant, College of Continuing Education, University of Minnesota

Here are some questions, in no particular order, that adults should consider before returning to school. Why are you thinking about going back to school? What is your goal, and will going back to school really help you achieve this goal? This is especially true when it comes to making career changes. If you're a career changer you should research the field you want to get into and find out what will make you competitive in that field. Some questions to ask are: Is there a preferred major? After assessing your skills and experiences, do you have gaps that your education will help to fill in? What can you do while in school through internships or other related experiences that will make you more competitive in the job market? Do you need a credential or can you gain skills via non-credit options?

What specific issues are important to you in going back to school? For example, consider cost, location, length of the program, how the program fits with your overall goals, quality of the program or institution, full versus part-time options, classroom versus distance learning options and financial aid.

You should also consider your current circumstances and constraints. Be honest with yourself about the tradeoffs that you may have to make. What kind of support will you need from family, friends and your employer and co-workers? Speak with these people, as appropriate, about the type of support you will need and what changes you and they may experience when you go back to school.

Think about your learning style and how you learn best, as well as any academic support you may need, which may include brushing up on writing, taking a study skills course, arranging for an orientation to the library or getting help with test anxiety.

Denise Rodak
Academic Advisor for the Center for Adult Learning, Montclair State University

First, students need to consider their ultimate motivation for returning to school. Is it to advance in their current position or to change careers? Is it for personal enrichment? Is it to finish something that they may have started some time ago? Having a clear motivation will not only help the student, but it will also help the academic advisor guide the student in terms of selecting a major, choosing classes and developing a realistic timetable for completion of the degree.

Students also need to realize that returning to school is going to require a commitment, both in terms of time and money. When considering the time commitment, it is important students not only take into account the actual "seat time," but also the amount of time they will need to complete assignments and study for exams. In terms of the financial commitment, students must find out exactly how much returning to school is going to cost. Many students only look at the per credit tuition cost and do not realize that they will also be responsible for any applicable fees such as parking, the student union and technology. Students should also factor in textbook costs, as well as any additional "wear and tear" on their automobile or public transportation expenses.

Finally, the decision to return to school will not only impact the student but also those around him or her. Prospective students should discuss the decision with family members, employers and even friends. I believe having a strong support network is critical to success in the classroom. Before starting school, a student needs to sit down and think of any potential conflicts such as time, space or money and who can help them resolve the conflicts.

Mary Kay Cooper
Director of Admissions and Adult Student Services, Seton Hill University

Starting school as an adult or going back to school as an adult is a HUGE deal for the people involved. Usually, by the time an admission professional sees a student, that student has done a lot of soul-searching. Most adults know that an undergraduate or graduate degree or certificate will open doors to new opportunities. Frequently these people have been told at work that they cannot be promoted or receive any more raises until they further their education. Often adults want to change careers and cannot do so unless they become educated in the new field. So it is not an issue of "Is education worthwhile?" but "Are the benefits of education worth the stresses this will cause for my family and me?"

Q. What do you say to students who think it's too late to go back to school?

Genelle Gatsos
Associate Director of Continuing Education, Susquehanna University

It is NEVER too late. The important thing is to focus on what you love to do and find a way to do it. In reality, most of us are going to be working well past traditional retirement age, so we have many years of working life ahead. It only makes sense then that the age to attend school would increase as well.

Q. What factors should adult students consider when selecting a school?

Denise Rodak
Academic Advisor for the Center for Adult Learning, Montclair State University

My number one tip for students returning to school is to do your research. The decision to obtain a degree should be treated like any other "major purchase" decision like buying a car or home. In order to make a successful "purchase," students need to be sure they and the school are a good fit. The following questions should be answered before starting at a college or university:

1. Does the school have the major I want to study?

2. Does the school offer courses for this major during the times in which I am free?

3. How much is the total cost?

4. Will my previous credits be accepted?

5. Who will I go to if I have questions?

6. How long will it take me to get to the school from my home or work?

7. What type of academic calendar does the school follow, such as semesters, trimesters or quarters?

I would also advise students to make sure they have a strong support network in place. Students receive encouragement from a number of different areas, both inside and outside the college or university. Family members, friends, supervisors, co-workers, academic advisors, faculty members and administrators are just a few of the people who can help a student achieve academic success simply by being a part of the support network.

Many colleges and universities also have organizations specifically designed to meet the needs of the adult student. At Montclair State University, the Non-Traditional Student Organization is part of the Student Government Organization, and they provide programming for the students as well as their family and friends. I would strongly advise any returning adult student to get involved in such an organization if offered at their institution.

Mary Kay Cooper
Director of Admissions and Adult Student Services, Seton Hill University

Students should begin by looking for programs that match their needs and aspirations. After determining how far a student is willing to commute, she needs to locate schools within that radius. This can be done by searching the Internet, consulting road maps and reading college guidebooks. If a student is changing career fields, he may need to search for a particular degree program. Sometimes I talk to students who "just need a bachelor's degree" to get promoted. If this is the case, and a particular academic discipline is not required, students should search for universities based on other criteria: location, cost or scheduling, for example. The same can be said if a student is going to school for personal enrichment.

Scheduling is often one of the most important issues adult students need to be concerned with. If an adult works 9 to 5, five days a week, obviously courses three days a week at 10 a.m. are not appropriate. Luckily, there is now a plethora of adult-friendly degree schedules. At Seton Hill University, we call this Work-Aware Scheduling. Programs for adults are offered online, in the evenings and on weekends. And often universities will have accelerated schedules so students come to campus only a few times per week but stay for many hours at a time. The days when adult students needed to spend a decade pursing a degree are over!

Prospective students should also attempt to find schools that offer services to adults. Students should ask the admission office, "Is there a College of Continuing Education?" At Seton Hill, we have an Office of Graduate and Adult Studies. Students should also ask practical questions such as: Are administration offices open in the evenings and on weekends? Is food available during adults' class times? Are procedures in place with the billing office to seamlessly process employer reimbursement of tuition? Are faculty willing to advise students over the phone or via email?

Finally, students who have previous college credits will want to inquire about how many of their credits will transfer. Students should also ask how many credits they need to complete their degree. If a degree program is 120 credits and the student transfers in 60 credits, the assumption should NOT be that the student only needs 60 credits to graduate. Universities may transfer in elective credits while credits for the major might still need to be taken. This information may help students narrow down the list of where they want to attend.

Unfortunately, most universities will only perform an "official" evaluation of transfer credits AFTER a student has applied and been accepted to the university. You should still ask for an "unofficial" evaluation before applying. Adult students are often concerned with how long it will take for them to earn their degree. Knowing how many credits still need to be taken helps in that planning. In addition, admission professionals can guide students toward other ways to shorten their stay at college, like "testing out" of certain courses or earning credits for life learning.

Dr. Lee Bash
Dean of the Division of Lifelong Learning, Baldwin-Wallace College

The market for adult learners has never been more competitive than it is today. And that competition shows no sign of diminishing. For adults, this should mean that finding the best fit should be easier than ever before. The main task before selecting a school is to make a list of all possible schools in the area that provide adult programs and determine the strengths and weaknesses for each. Convenience is a primary consideration. How close is each school to work or home? What about reputation? Some schools may be cheaper but if their product is inferior—and if they don't have a solid reputation, having a degree from such a school may reflect poorly on the student—it's no bargain. This investigation needs to be thorough. For instance, in the area surrounding Cleveland, there are a number of schools that offer all their classes as five-week courses and make a big deal about it. However, when you do the math in terms of maximum hours to be completed in one year, other schools with other formats offer as many or even more hours while the outcomes from the courses may reflect even better learning. So adult learners really need to fully weigh all options.

Q. What other benefits should adult students look for when selecting a program?

Genelle Gatsos
Associate Director of Continuing Education, Susquehanna University

When are classes scheduled? Are the times compatible with job and family responsibilities? What is the registration and application process like? Students often end up discouraged by the bureaucracy of the process. Look for a program that simplifies the process. Is advising available? Academic advising can help students avoid taking unnecessary classes. Also, look for any special needs that you have. Some schools, for example, may have childcare facilities available to students.

Dr. Charles Curry
Director of the Adult Degree Program, James Madison University

Providing support services for returning adult students is critical for successful adult programs. We have limited financial resources but have used the volunteer human resources of our graduates to provide many support services including starting a mentorship program, a portfolio-pizza night, classroom resource persons, an online silent auction, a welcome aboard barbeque, an awards banquet, senior project forums and promotion and marketing persons.

Deborah S. Gwin
Director, UA Adult Focus, University of Akron

We think the effort we put forth to assist adults is unique and important for their academic success. We offer special orientation sessions for adults to address their specific concerns and a "Transitions" workshop on Saturdays. We have a Mentoring Program that raises our retention rate significantly in the mentored group, Learning Communities during the day and evening and a series of academic skills workshops based on adult learning theory. One workshop is called "Focus on Success" and is given in the evenings and Saturdays.

Q. Should students consider cost when looking at schools?

Mary Kay Cooper
Director of Admissions and Adult Student Services, Seton Hill University

Students should not strike colleges from their lists based on cost. Private schools cost more than public schools but frequently have more financial aid to offer. Although cost is one of the first things students ask about, it should, in reality, be one of the last items to consider in the decision-making process. A student may be able to afford an expensive institution but will never know that unless she begins the process toward finding that out.

Q. What are the advantages and disadvantages of a certificate program, associate's degree or bachelor's degree?

Donna DeSpain
Director of Adult and Graduate Studies, Aurora University
We use certificate programs as a way for adult students to improve their marketable skills and to also serve as an entree into higher education. The associate's degree serves some students as the ticket they need to improve their position in the job market. For others, it serves as the courage for them to seek a full-fledged bachelor's degree.

Q. What should students know about taking online courses?

Mary Kay Cooper
Director of Admissions and Adult Student Services, Seton Hill University
Taking courses online can be quite tempting to working, adult students, and online courses are certainly valuable. However students should be aware of the extraordinary discipline required to be successful in online courses. Students should examine their work habits to determine their level of discipline. Are they procrastinators? Do they work well with deadlines? Do they need someone "standing over them" to accomplish their work? Regardless of the student's level of discipline, I would advise students to take a couple of traditional, on-site courses before attempting an online course.

Q. What qualities do you look for in selecting students? How are these qualities different from traditional students?

Kristine Rabberman
Director of Liberal Arts Programs, College of General Studies, University of Pennsylvania
The College of General Studies' admission decisions are made by different committees than those that make admission decisions for Penn's College of Arts and Sciences. At

CGS, we look for evidence of past academic achievement through high school and college transcripts, and we review students' writing in their admission essays, both to see how well they write and also to see how focused and clear their academic goals are. We request a resume and give students an opportunity in one essay to describe any non-academic experience such as employment, community affairs, volunteer work or publications that strengthens their application. We also weight recent transcripts more heavily than we do earlier transcripts. Finally, we do not require SAT scores from undergraduate applicants, nor are MLA (Master of Liberal Arts) applicants required to submit GRE scores. We find standardized tests to be poor predictors of how adult students will perform in the classroom. We do require international students to submit TOEFL scores, however. In general, we are aware that maturity, focus, time management and organizational skills are important to adult students' success in the classroom, and we are also aware that research and writing experience gained in the workplace or through volunteer activities can give adult learners a strong foundation for their academic work.

Deborah S. Gwin
Director, UA Adult Focus, University of Akron

The University of Akron is an open admission, public metropolitan institution. Thus, we require only a high school diploma or GED for admission—and a pulse. (Excuse the admission humor.) We offer first-generation-college, low-income and under-prepared adults the opportunity to better themselves and their life situation through higher education. We tell them that higher education is the single most important factor toward financial independence. The adult students who succeed here are highly motivated and have a wonderful capacity for perseverance.

Dr. Lee Bash
Dean of the Division of Lifelong Learning, Baldwin-Wallace College

The qualities we value in our adult learners are somewhat subjective but highly observable. We look for motivation, a strong sense of purpose, good communication skills, maturity, energy and the ability to persevere. I mention these attributes first because we frequently encounter an adult learner whose previous college experiences, typically more than 10 years earlier, were marginal or unsuccessful. If our only criteria were based on such evidence, we would miss the opportunity to work with some of our best students now. These students demonstrate motivation and a strong sense of purpose. At the same time, there are two qualities that I believe support success among students better than any others: writing and organization skills.

Because Baldwin-Wallace College is a private school with a strong liberal arts core curriculum, we understand that selectivity is a part of our identity. Adult learners who come to us tend to have a sense that they are seeking a value-added education and they can usually articulate the advantages associated with their studies here rather than somewhere else. They may not always understand the full implications of a liberal arts education, but they tend to respond to our reputation and our responsiveness to their unique needs. We see this as an issue of "fit"—where the students and we have identified a set of values that provide a strong match that may even justify additional sacrifices as long as the students believe the benefits outweigh the costs.

Dr. Charles Curry
Director of the Adult Degree Program, James Madison University

At James Madison University we have an open door policy for returning adult students who have had a lapse of at least three years in their post-secondary education and who have accumulated at least 30 semester hours of credit that can be used in their bachelor's degree program. We have found that returning adult students are a highly motivated group and that previous academic records are not indicative of future academic performance. We do not require submission of high school records or SAT or ACT test scores. Our adults have an average GPA of 3.4 on a 4.0 scale.

Q. What might adult students be surprised to learn about what you want when selecting students for your program?

Denise Rodak
Academic Advisor for the Center for Adult Learning, Montclair State University

Students might be surprised to learn the importance of the essay questions. Not only are we interested in determining if the applicant can follow directions and construct a well-written essay, but we are also very interested in the actual answers.

Our essay questions deal specifically with an applicant's motivation for returning to school, as well as whether or not he or she has thought about any necessary accommodations that may need to be made. The person reviewing the essays is looking to see that the applicant has considered these two points and is ready to make the commitment.

Frances Markunas
Associate Dean and Director of Strategic Alliances, College of Continuing Studies, Rider University

The biggest surprise for adult students is how easy it is to apply, have transcripts evaluated, receive credit for prior learning and register for courses that are offered in multiple formats for their convenience. The hardest step is getting the courage to contact us. After that the CCS staff walks everyone through the process, which can be as simple as completing a one-page application with a $40 application fee.

Q. What is your selection process? What happens to an application once it is received by your office?

Kristine Rabberman
Director of Liberal Arts Programs, College of General Studies, University of Pennsylvania

Undergraduate applicants need to submit a completed application, including a list of post-secondary schools attended and application essays, an official high school transcript if the applicant has less than two years of liberal arts work at the college level, a GED score if the applicant has not completed high school, official transcripts for all colleges and universities attended and evidence of English language proficiency for international students via a TOEFL exam or an EPFS recommendation with Michigan Test scores. We also have several essays for students to complete. Students may also attach a resume.

Once an application is received, an academic advisor in the program reviews the application. If the applicant to a BA program has a 3.0 GPA in previous course work and strong essays, the advisor can simply admit the student. If the student does not meet these qualifications, the advisor presents the application at a weekly admissions committee meeting, attended by other undergraduate advisors and chaired by the director of Liberal Arts Programs. At this time, the committee will weigh other factors such as extracurricular experience and quality of essays and will vote as a committee whether to accept a student as a full admit or provisional admit, defer the decision pending receipt of new information, such as additional courses taken at another institution or reject the applicant.

Master of Liberal Arts applicants need to submit an application with application essays, official transcripts from every college or university attended, two letters of recommendation from academic or personal references and an admission interview with an MLA advisor. Applicants are not required to take the GRE. We look to see that applicants have the academic qualifications needed to do well in graduate work at Penn and an idea for an interdisciplinary concentration in the liberal arts. An admission committee made up of the MLA advisor and the director of Liberal Arts Programs considers all applications. If the applicant to the MLA program has a 3.0 GPA in previous course work in the liberal arts and strong essays, the committee simply admits the student. If the student does not meet these qualifications, the committee will weigh other factors such as extracurricular experience and quality of essays and will vote as a committee.

We have rolling admission, so we accept students to the fall, spring and summer terms, and we can accept any student who is qualified to be in our programs. As soon as we make an admission, we generate a letter specifying our decision and notify the student.

Q. What is the best way to make sure that students get the most credits transferred?

Janet Pelto
Lifework Consultant, College of Continuing Education, University of Minnesota

If you think some credits should have transferred that didn't, ask to review the school's transfer of credit policy to see if the school overlooked something in the transfer credit evaluation. Note that credits from a technical program or proprietary school may not transfer to all colleges and universities. If you are taking courses now that you want to transfer in the future, it is best that you work with the school you hope to transfer to and find out what you should take now and make sure it will transfer. Every school has its own requirements, and what fulfills a requirement at one school may only transfer to another as an elective.

Genelle Gatsos
Associate Director of Continuing Education, Susquehanna University

The best way is to have your previous college transcript evaluated early on to see exactly where you stand. Often it is necessary to provide course descriptions or syllabi for classes taken. I think it is worth the extra effort to get this additional information. It can mean more approved transfer credit, which can lead to a substantial savings in time and money.

Q. Do old credits ever expire?

Frances Markunas
Associate Dean and Director of Strategic Alliances, College of Continuing Studies, Rider University

Old credit policies vary from institution to institution. For example, Rider's is as follows: "The academic record of a student returning to Rider after an absence of 10 years or more will be re-evaluated to determine the applicability of old courses to present requirements...Old courses that are judged applicable to current degree programs will be used to meet degree requirements." Within the College of Continuing Studies, our Bachelor of Arts in Liberal Studies allows us the greatest flexibility to accept transfer credits.

Janet Pelto
Lifework Consultant, College of Continuing Education, University of Minnesota

Generally, undergraduate credits do not expire. However, if a field has changed dramatically since you took the course, you may need to retake it. This is a decision made by the individual school or program. Generally, graduate-level credits expire after seven years, but every institution has its own guidelines.

Q. What tips do you have for adult students to get the best recommendations possible?

Kristine Rabberman
Director of Liberal Arts Programs, College of General Studies, University of Pennsylvania

We require recommendations for our MLA program, but BA candidates can also submit letters of recommendation if they wish. Academic references are always nice, but since many of our applicants have been out of school for a while, we are comfortable accepting professional references. On the other hand, references from family friends and relatives are not appropriate. It is best for recommenders to think about some qualities or skills that would be important in the classroom. Transferable skills include writing and communication skills, research experience, time management skills, intellectual curiosity, integrity, focus, commitment and organizational skills. Lukewarm, generic letters and short, overly effusive letters don't make much of an impact on us. We prefer honest letters and ones that include one or two specific examples to illustrate a positive quality of the applicant. It's a good idea for students to share with their recommenders their ideas on how their academic program will fit into their lives so recommenders can write letters tailored to our programs.

Q. Since you don't require an essay, what is the best way that students can convey their individual strengths?

Dr. Lee Bash
Dean of the Division of Lifelong Learning, Baldwin-Wallace College

B-W doesn't require an essay for admission, though we often interview students we suspect might be marginal or have notable challenges with their studies. One of the primary attributes I look for is determination. That's something that comes through in any form of communication. In our introductory course, we cite research that suggests a high correlation between perseverance and success. In fact, perseverance is the highest predictor of success. For many of our students, this simply reinforces what they already believe though for some, it articulates something they may have only felt intuitively before.

Q. What are the qualities of a good admission essay?

Kristine Rabberman
Director of Liberal Arts Programs, College of General Studies, University of Pennsylvania

While we ask such questions as whether the students want to explain any aspects of their transcripts or academic record, we primarily provide questions that ask students to describe their plans for study at Penn and how those plans fit into their overall lives. We are not interested in having students write about how wonderful Penn is. Instead, we want to see prose that is clear, focused and articulate. We want the students to honestly describe themselves and their motivations for study. If students have any problematic patterns in their transcripts such as low grades, incompletes or withdrawals, it is always best for them to give some explanation. It is important for students to write their essays themselves, since good writing skills are required in courses at Penn. Students need to spend time on their essays and proofread carefully.

Q. What advice do you have for the essay?

Denise Rodak
Academic Advisor for the Center for Adult Learning, Montclair State University

Students applying to the university through the Center for Adult Learning must complete two essay questions as part of the application process. My first, and most important, piece of advice for a student is simply to read the directions. Our essays have very specific instructions in terms of length, margins, spacing and font including type size. While the directions are not difficult, I am amazed at how many applicants do not take the time to read these instructions. Following directions is critical to success in the classroom, and the people reviewing the applications want to see that prospective students take the time to read the instructions and complete the essays as directed.

I would also advise students to treat the essay as though it was their first "assignment." This means writing a clear, well-organized essay that is grammatically correct, with no errors in spelling, punctuation or capitalization. Our reviewers want to see that the applicant put both thought and time into the essay.

Q. Are there essay topics that don't work?

Mary Kay Cooper
Director of Admissions and Adult Student Services, Seton Hill University

Seton Hill University does not require an essay for admission to its adult, undergraduate programs. Most of our graduate programs do require what we call a Letter of Intent. Some universities will require specific content for the essay. For example, "Please submit a letter of intent demonstrating career goals that are consistent with program outcomes and goals." Regardless of how structured the topic is, students should take the essay seriously and write truthfully.

Not only does the student want to make sure she matches with the university, but the university wants to make sure the student is a good match for the program. The essay may help in this regard. Essay topics should be conservative and professional. Remember several complete strangers may be reading this essay and then meeting the student in person afterwards. An essay on how the student's first mammogram experience made her want to become a physician assistant may not be the best way to go! After the student completes the first draft of the essay, proofread, proofread, proofread! Then the student should give the essay to a colleague or friend to proofread, again.

Q. Does your school offer scholarships for adult students? Are they need-based, merit-based or both? Are they available for part-time students as well?

Fran Van Slyke-Zaslofsky
Financial Aid Coordinator, College of Continuing Education Student Services and Advising at the University of Minnesota, Twin Cities

University of Minnesota College of Continuing Education (CCE) scholarships require both merit and need and are available to CCE adult learners who are enrolled in a broad range of educational courses and programs. Non-admitted students enrolled in credit courses, degree and certificate admits and students enrolled in noncredit continuing professional education and personal enrichment courses are eligible. Adults need flexible scholarship criteria that include basing eligibility on current income rather than on previous tax year income, which is used for mainstream financial aid programs. We define need broadly, taking into account factors like disability issues, previous access to education, time available for paid employment, demands of juggling multiple roles of work, family and community. We also assess other indicators of ability or potential to succeed beyond the academic record, including credentials or certifications, skills, paid or unpaid work experience, leadership, problem-solving ability, initiative, perseverance and the ability to set realistic and attainable goals. All of this goes into the determination process of who receives scholarships from the college.

Kristine Rabberman
Director of Liberal Arts Programs, College of General Studies, University of Pennsylvania

We offer scholarships for undergraduate students. They are both need-based and merit-based and are restricted to part-time students. Updated scholarship information is posted on our website at http://www.sas.upenn.edu/CGS/undergraduate/scholarships.php.

Dr. Charles Curry
Director of the Adult Degree Program, James Madison University

We have a very active alumni chapter that is dedicated to supporting adult students who are earning their degrees. Our alumni chapter has endowed a $25,000 scholarship that is available as a merit-based scholarship. Nearly all of our students are part-time students and employed full time. All of the financial aid is available to either full- or part-time students.

Donna DeSpain
Director of Adult and Graduate Studies, Aurora University

Scholarships are available for full-time adult students. These full-time students are eligible to apply for merit grants and for state and federal funds. Part-time students are generally not eligible for grants but are eligible for state and federal funds.

Q. What are some of the best sources of money for college for adult students?

Fran Van Slyke-Zaslofsky
Financial Aid Coordinator, College of Continuing Education Student Services and Advising at the University of Minnesota, Twin Cities

Some of the best sources include employer tuition benefits, Dislocated Worker Programs, AmeriCorps awards, federal education tax credits and deductions, such as Lifetime Learning Tax Credits and deductions for eligible higher education expenses and scholarships administered on students' campuses or in their communities that have flexible eligibility criteria.

Q. What don't adult students know that they should know about paying for their educations?

Fran Van Slyke-Zaslofsky
Financial Aid Coordinator, College of Continuing Education Student
Services and Advising at the University of Minnesota, Twin Cities

Adult learners have many misconceptions about financial aid, including that it is only for graduating high school seniors going directly to college. Some also believe that aid is only available to students admitted to a degree program and enrolled full-time. Students need to realize that there are many ways to pay for their education that go beyond mainstream federal, state and institutional grants, scholarships, loans and work-study. Resources include government agencies such as VA benefits, AmeriCorps and Dislocated Worker Programs, scholarships from community, religious and professional organizations, federal education tax credits and deductions, tuition installment options, credit card payment and college savings plans.

There is a lot of information on the Web, but it is very fragmented. Adults need tools to manage it and figure out which aid programs fit their individual situations. Adults in non-traditional programs have an especially difficult time sorting through the bewildering array of options.

Additionally, students who have already earned a bachelor's or advanced degree often become discouraged because their degrees may not be marketable, and they see an abundance of aid programs for students working on their first degrees. Although their options are more limited, they do have options and they need to know what they are.

We have developed a Financial Resources Wizard for adult learners at the University of Minnesota, Twin Cities. It is an interactive web tool that asks users a series of questions and identifies options that match the user's situation: http://www.cce.umn.edu/financialaid. Although it includes some programs specific to the U of M, Twin Cities, it can be used by students at other institutions to get the "lay of the land" and give them ideas about possible sources of funding.

Deborah S. Gwin
Director, UA Adult Focus, University of Akron

There is a huge information gap in this arena. It seems there are some adults here who are literally incensed that they must pay for their schooling at all. Many think they can submit the Free Application For Federal Student Aid (FAFSA) a month or so before the beginning of the semester and have everything taken care of. They have no idea about the cost of textbooks and think they can wait for their Stafford Loans to arrive on the 30th day of the semester before buying their books. I have had students who think we should provide them with home computers and even food, at no cost, as if the university were some sort of social service agency. On the other hand, adult students often do not think they are eligible for scholarships. To address these misconceptions we have compiled a large notebook here of scholarship opportunities for adult learners and encourage them to apply. We have had several excellent successes! We also administer a privately funded scholarship for displaced homemakers.

Q. What are strategies for adult students to succeed in the classroom?

Dr. James M. Sloat
Director of the Center for Learning and Teaching, Washington and Jefferson College

1. Be confident. Yes, the classroom may seem like a foreign land, but you bring a great deal with you. Adult students have an experience base that is invaluable in the classroom. They have a great deal to contribute, and they should be active in doing so. They should remember that they are smarter than they think they are, and they should make connections between the ideas that they are encountering in the classroom and their experiences in life.

2. Be prepared. Adult students are making an effort to learn something new. In most cases, this effort involves some amount of sacrifice of both time and money. The best way to maximize the payoff from the sacrifice is to prepare for class. Doing the relevant readings before class will enable the student to both understand the material more thoroughly and to identify questions or areas of uncertainty. The student is then able to ask the instructor for clarification. Over half of the classroom battle is won before the class ever begins; it is important to be prepared. For adult students, this often requires blocking aside specific times and places for studying. While this may not be easy due to the variety of other commitments, it is essential for success in the classroom.

3. Be strategic. When preparing for examinations, students should be strategic. They should put themselves in their professors' positions and ask what questions they would ask if they were constructing the test. By studying strategically and preparing responses to those anticipated questions, students put themselves in the best position to succeed. Getting together with other students–perhaps other adult students–in the class can be a helpful way to fill in gaps in one's notes and to discuss the material outside of the classroom.

Janet Pelto
Lifework Consultant, College of Continuing Education, University of Minnesota

While adults typically do well when they go back to school, starting with one course is usually a good way to "ease back into it." Most adults working full time take one, maybe two, courses per term. You should start with something you are interested in and in which you think you will do well. By doing this, you can "try on" returning to school before you actually commit to an entire program. It's a good idea for you to take a course to see what it will be like for you to be a student again, as part of your decision-making process to go back to school.

While most adults are apprehensive about going back to school, most do very well academically. The skills they use every day are the skills that will enable them to be good students, such as time management, the abilities to prioritize and multi-task and the willingness to ask questions. They often enjoy being back in school. Professors appreciate having adults in the classroom because they are more willing to participate in discussions, bring in new ideas and make connections that enrich the experience for everyone.

Q. What are the most common mistakes that students make when returning to school?

Dr. James M. Sloat
Director of the Center for Learning and Teaching, Washington and Jefferson College

1. The comparison game. When adult students start saying, "When I was a student, no one ever..." or, "Students today just don't understand..." While there may indeed be some discernable and interesting differences between the classroom experience then and now, dwelling on these differences is rarely productive and often creates resentment. Realize that younger students may not be able to do some of the long division in their heads, but they can likely gather research on the Internet very effectively. At the heart of collaborative learning is mutual respect. By practicing such respect, adult learners may be surprised by how much they can learn from their younger colleagues.

2. The soapbox. Some adult learners see the classroom as their own personal platform for making pronouncements about a variety of issues. While one's experiences and perspectives are certainly valuable, they should always be framed in the context of the course material. Adult students should know that some professors harbor concerns about being upstaged. Fellow students also are not fond of being preached at. As long as adult students focus on the course material, limit any editorializing and share the participation time with the other students, they can expect to find a welcoming environment for class participation.

3. Wasted opportunities. Adult learners generally have a set of responsibilities and obligations that far exceed those of 18 to 22 year olds. Since most professors in traditional college settings design their courses with traditional students in mind, they may not design their assignments in ways that are immediately compatible with a job, childcare responsibilities and household chores. As a result, some adult students end up being overwhelmed by the workload and devoting only the time that they can spare once the responsibilities have been fulfilled. Too often, the time available is insufficient for the demands of the course. It is important for adult learners

to reserve time and space for reading, studying, homework and other assignments. Otherwise, the opportunity of going to school may be squandered.

Donna DeSpain
Director of Adult and Graduate Studies, Aurora University
The two most common mistakes that I've observed in working with adult students is that they do not understand the funding opportunities available to them and they do not realize the level of organization that they will need to employ to realize success in school.

Dr. Charles Curry
Director of the Adult Degree Program, James Madison University
The most common mistake is not making their return to school a high enough priority. Going to school is almost never the number one priority for an adult student as it is for most traditional students. For adult students to be successful, however, it must be one of their highest priorities because there are almost always barriers, frustrations and time constraints that must be overcome.

Q. What advice do you have for students to balance their studies, families and maybe even jobs?

Dr. Lee Bash
Dean of the Division of Lifelong Learning, Baldwin-Wallace College
School for adults is about a lot more than simple "book-learning." The first step I recommend is that adult learners sit down with their families to discuss the major lifestyle change they are about to encounter. There are horror stories associated with families or loved ones who not only don't support an adult learner, but they actually sabotage them. In the best of circumstances, the family works as a support group, everyone buys into the adult learner's quest and does whatever it takes to share the burden and provide assistance.

There are at least two other considerations that adults need to cultivate if they are going to be successful: time management skills and stress management. Students who ignore these areas do so at their own risk with a significantly higher likelihood of ultimately failing. These are topics any adult learner needs to address, understand, practice and become adept at. They need not be prescriptive since each student can identify what works best for himself or herself, but any student who isn't intentional in developing these areas isn't exercising much wisdom.

Along with this comes the ability to honestly self-assess. I see examples of students who take on too much–in some cases, their urgency becomes overwhelming or they don't provide any margin for error or any unforeseen factor, but they end up being their own worst enemy. In most cases, this can simply be addressed by sometimes saying "no" and always being vigilant about overextending.

Mary Kay Cooper
Director of Admissions and Adult Student Services, Seton Hill University

Adults going to college provide good modeling for their children, co-workers and staff. However, it takes some balance to do well. Chores should be re-distributed at home. If resources are available, students should consider hiring a housekeeper or landscaper to work in the home or yard every couple of weeks. If the adult student is in a program where she goes to school every Saturday, then it should become widely known at work and home that "Saturday is my class day." Events should be planned around class day, for example. Although students may need to scale back the time involvement, hobbies should be maintained as much as possible for mental health. Plus students deprived of fun make for very unhappy students. The bottom line mentality, though, should always be that school is a "temporary discomfort with tremendous long-term benefits." Students should explain to their families what benefits they'll see in the future when the program is completed, like increased income or more job possibilities. And all in all, achieving this goal will make for a happier mom, dad or spouse!

Create A Winning Application

Getting Admitted Should Not Be A Mystery

When you imagine how colleges decide which students to admit and which to reject, you might picture a table surrounded by faceless, dark figures. You may even fear these anonymous admission officers who have the power to cast away applications simply on a whim. "Too old," one exclaims as he dumps the application into the trashcan. "Weak academic record," says another as she crumples and tosses the application onto the floor.

While it would be much more exciting to write about if the above were true, it is, fortunately, not. The truth is that every admission officer who we've met (and we've met hundreds) has a similar approach to reviewing applications. They are looking for reasons to admit students, not to deny them. Admission officers carefully review every application looking for signs that the applicant is a fit for the college and would make a successful student.

While admission officers strive to be fair and balanced, they have no qualms about rejecting applicants who thoughtlessly scribble answers on their applications and who don't take the process seriously. For schools where there are more applicants than seats in the classroom, competition can be fierce which means you'll definitely want to spend time on your application to make sure it is as strong as possible.

The first step to creating a successful college application is to understand how the process works and what admission officers are looking for when reviewing your application. Once you know how the process works, you can begin to market yourself to the college, showing them why you deserve to be there.

How The Admission Process Works

Colleges are a lot like nightclubs. Some are open to anyone who can pay the cover charge. Others have velvet ropes and bouncers to carefully select who to admit. For less selective programs like community colleges or certificate programs, you may only need to complete an application form and meet the minimum requirements, and you'll be automatically admitted. For more selective programs, you'll need to complete an application form, which may include writing an essay, getting recommendation letters and even doing an interview.

For these more selective programs, your application will be reviewed by the admission office. Some schools even have special admission officers who specialize in adult applicants. Usually if two admission officers recommend accepting you, an admission director signs off on the recommendations and you are accepted. At other schools, admission officers make recommendations to an admission committee, which then decides as a group whether to accept, deny or defer your application.

In terms of deadlines, some colleges have a single deadline for all applications. Other schools have a priority deadline for students who want to be considered for both admission and financial aid and then a later deadline for students who just want to be considered for admission. Finally, some schools have what is known as rolling admission, which means that the college will accept students until they fill up all of the open spaces. In every case it is critical that you understand when the deadline is, and in most cases, the sooner you submit your application the better.

Putting Together A Compelling Application

Let's assume that you are applying to a college or university that does not accept every applicant. This means that you will fill out an application that includes lists of your accomplishments, previous educational experience, personal essays and letters of recommendation, and you may even have an interview. It might be useful to think of the entire application as a puzzle. Your job is to fit together the different pieces of your life including your work experience and personal and professional goals to show the college why you deserve to be admitted.

In this and the following chapters we'll examine each piece of the application and explore how to best showcase your strengths. Let's start with the first piece of the puzzle, the application form.

The Application Form

The application form appears fairly straightforward. Besides the basic information such as your name and address, you need to list your accomplishments, past education, work experience, awards and activities. The reason colleges ask for this information is to better gauge what your experiences have been, what kind of person you are and how going back to school fits into your goals for the future. Ultimately, they are not only getting to know you better but also evaluating whether you have the drive and commitment to be a successful student. So let's dive into each area of the application form.

Accomplishments. Adults often get tripped up by applications that ask for your accomplishments. After all, you've long ago packed away your trophies and ribbons from high school, and the "Mom or Dad of the Year" certificate that your kid handcrafted is not exactly what colleges mean. Fortunately, colleges don't expect you to list things like Noble or Pulitzer prizes as accomplishments. They expect much more humble accomplishments. For many of these, you don't even need a ribbon or certificate to demonstrate their merit. Take a look at the following questions to help you draw out your accomplishments:

- If you have previous college experience, what notable projects or papers did you do? Did you conduct any research?

- At work have you ever been recognized for specific contributions or meeting specific goals?

- Has your boss singled you out for special recognition for a specific accomplishment?

- Have you taken a work-related class or workshop?

- What are you most proud of accomplishing at work?

- Have you volunteered?

- Do you have any hobbies or interests?

- Have you ever been written about in the local newspaper for your skills, interests or hobbies?

- Have you ever taught any subject even if informally? For example, you may have led a scrap-booking workshop at church.

- Do you play recreational sports? Have you competed in a tournament or competition?

- What special skills have you learned? Can you claim a mastery of a skill like sewing, photography, foreign languages, etc.?

- Have you taken a class, workshop or seminar for fun?

- Are you a leader in any organization?

- Have you led a special project for any of the groups you belong to? For example, you may have organized a fundraiser for your child's soccer team.

- In terms of your family, what are you most proud of having accomplished? For example, you might be proud of the fact that you manage your family's day-to-day finances or that you were able to save up money to send your kids through college.

- If your family were to give you an award, what would it be for?

As you can see you have a lot of latitude when describing your accomplishments. Don't limit yourself by thinking that accomplishments always have to be accompanied by an award or certificate. You can share any accomplishment that you are proud of. It can be related to work, family or even a hobby.

Academic Background. In the application forms you'll need to describe your academic background, including degrees you've earned and college courses you've taken. This information is pretty straightforward so there is not a lot of word tweaking that you will need to do to detail your academic background.

What's important is that you don't forget any of your educational experiences. Remember to include all of the courses that you took, even if they were several years ago or weekend, evening or summer courses.

But what if you did horribly in high school or college? Fortunately, most schools won't view your grades from high school or even college as being indicative of your academic potential. Colleges understand that there are many reasons why a student would not get good grades that are totally unrelated to their academic abilities. Plus, many years may have passed since you went to high school or college. For most schools, there is an informal statute of limitation on your grades. If you did poorly in the past, don't worry about that preventing your getting a second chance today. Most schools look instead at your more recent work or personal experiences and your reasons for going back to school.

Work. What's more important than the number of years that you have worked or your job title is what you did during that time. In other words, the quality of your work is more important than the quantity.

When describing your work, don't just provide a job description of what you've done. It's better to explain what you accomplished in a position. Here's an example of two ways to describe the same job:

```
Sales manager. Managed sales of software and
maintained customer relations.

Sales manager. Managed software sales. In-
creased volume by 25 percent and customer
retention by 15 percent.
```

Do you see how the second description does more than provide a job description? Rather than just explaining your responsibilities, it gives context to what you accomplished in your role as a sales manager. As you review your career at work, think about how you can highlight your accomplishments in a measurable way. This will help you distinguish what you've accomplished at work.

It might be helpful to take some time to think about your experiences. Did you manage others, lead a project or head a committee? Did you make a measurable contribution, receive recognition for your efforts or improve your working situation? Did you implement a new system? Did you train new employees? Did you increase sales or productivity? Were you promoted? It's important that you convey the results of your work experience to the colleges.

Volunteer Experience. If you volunteer, then you know how much personal satisfaction you can get from giving back to your community. You may not realize how much colleges and graduate schools value what you are doing as well. Many schools will ask about your volunteer experience because they know that in addition to helping others, you are learning valuable skills, some of which may be similar to on-the-job skills. This is especially important for students who do not work for pay.

Like work experience, for volunteer experience, it's also important to outline your contributions and what skills you may have learned. Take a look at these two descriptions:

```
Performing arts center volunteer: Volun-
teered 200 hours.
```

```
Performing arts center volunteer: Volun-
teered 200 hours. Learned about theatre man-
agement and event marketing.
```

Which one conveys more useful information to the admission officers? In the second description, the applicant shares not only how long she volunteered but also what she learned from the experience. If she plans to major in theatre, this is extremely important information. But even if she is not a theatre major, the organizational and management experiences are important skills for almost any major.

Honors And Awards. Colleges and graduate schools want to know about honors and awards that you've won to get an idea of how you have excelled. For example, at work you may have been named employee of the month, met your sales goals for the year or been noticed for community involvement. Or maybe your department won a group accolade for highest production levels, meeting deadlines or contributing to a special project.

Also, don't limit yourself to only work-related honors. You may have been recognized by your community, church, club or other organization. You may have had some of your poetry or writing published in a local paper. These kinds of honors are very important for colleges to know about.

As you are selecting awards to list, make sure that you provide context for them. In other words, don't just state which award you won, but explain the significance of it. Here's an example of an award with no context:

```
Employee of the month.
```

This does not tell us much about the award. What if there were only four employees in the entire company? So to give context you could write:

```
Employee of the month. Selected among 200
employees for highest level of customer ser-
vice.
```

You can see how the second description explains why the applicant was given the award and how much of an honor it was to be selected among 200 employees.

You can also list other honors such as:

```
Poetry published in "Community News," the
weekly newspaper of Jonestown.
```

Anything that recognizes your talents and skills is important to share with the college even if it is not an "award" in the traditional sense. This helps them understand that you not only participate in something but you excel in it as well.

Activities. Classes would be pretty boring if none of the students brought in their experiences outside of the classroom into the discussion. This is exactly why colleges and graduate schools want to know about your participation in activities. They know that what you learn outside of the classroom will enhance your learning experience in the classroom.

When you think about your activities, consider social, cultural, political and religious organizations in which you've participated. Don't overlook activities that are not formally organized. Even if you aren't a member of a club, you can list hobbies or recreational activities such as sewing, collecting or hiking.

Ideally, you can include activities that are related to your field of study. For example, if you are interested in environmental studies, then listing your participation in the Sierra Club or bird watching makes sense. These activities illustrate your passion for the outdoors and enhance your reasons for wanting to major in environmental studies. However, showing this kind of connection is not required, and it still helps the college admission officers understand who you are by sharing your activities.

When you write about your activities, you may think of them as just something fun that you do. But they are also a good way to show your strengths to the school. Try to show merit or leadership if you can. Have you accomplished something through the activity, been recognized for an achievement or dedicated a significant amount of time? Have you led other members of an organization, organized an event or started a special project? These are the measurable ways that you can reflect to the school your contribution to the activity.

As you are completing your applications, remember that you are not just filling out a form. You are creating a portrait of who you are and what you have to share with the school. That's why it's important that you spend the time to think about each item. Don't just list them, but explain what you've gained from the experience. That, more than anything else, will help the college or graduate school learn what you have to offer.

Standardized Tests

When you were in high school you may remember being tormented by the three-lettered tests, the SAT and ACT. Thankfully, most schools do not require that you take them if you are an adult student. Check with your school to make sure, but most likely you will be spared the three-hour exams.

However, while you may not need to take exams to gain admission to a college, you may need to take placement exams once you are admitted as a student. Some schools require that adult students take placement exams in writing and math to make sure that you are matched to the right level of classes.

And if you are applying to graduate school, you may need to take a standardized test for admission. For example, you may need to take the GRE (www.gre.org). If you are applying to a professional school, you will be required to take the GMAT for business school (www.gmac.com), LSAT for law school (www.lsac.org) or MCAT for medical school (www.aamc.org).

It may have been a while since you've taken a standardized test, which means that it's a good idea to do some preparation beforehand. You can prepare on your own or with some help. If you prepare on your own, get the exam guide from the test maker. This will explain the material that will be tested and the format of the exam and provide you with a sample exam to take. Most of the test makers also offer guides with additional tests that you can take for practice. This is one of the best ways to prepare, by taking old exams for practice.

If you need some help reviewing the material or some motivation to study, consider getting help to prepare for the exam. There are national and regional test preparation companies including Kaplan and Princeton Review that offer courses specifically designed to review for these standardized tests. Contact one of the companies to attend a free informational session to find out more about costs and what they'll provide.

FIVE

Craft An Admission Resume

Writing Your Admission Resume

If you wrote your autobiography, how long would it be? Perhaps several hundred pages including photographs of important people, places and events in your life. Now imagine condensing that autobiography into a single page. While it sounds impossible, that's exactly what a college or graduate school wants when it asks for a resume. Even if the college you are applying to doesn't explicitly ask for a resume we recommend that you include one with your application anyway.

Like a resume that you may have written when applying for a job, a college admission resume highlights your skills, accomplishments, talents and experience in a quick, easy-to-digest format. But unlike an employer, a college or graduate school is not concerned with your job titles as much as they are in the skills you learned on the job and how they will prepare you for your studies.

Let's dive in and take a look at what makes a good admission resume.

Resume Basics

If it's been a while since you've job hunted or your resume skills are a bit rusty, here's a primer on what goes into a good resume. Basically, you have one, maybe two, pages to summarize what you've accomplished. For an admission resume the schools will want you to focus on three major areas: your education, work experience and other relevant experiences.

For your education, you should list the institutions you've attended, the degrees that you've earned, your GPA and any honors you've received. Don't worry if you did poorly in college before. College admission officers know that you were younger then and weren't as focused on your studies, which is precisely why you are going back to school now.

For work experience, detail the companies you've worked at, the positions you've held and the major accomplishments you've made.

Don't forget to describe your responsibilities and any knowledge that you gained that might apply to your studies. For example, if you worked in sales and are planning to major in political science, you could certainly highlight your understanding of sales negotiations between buyers and sellers, which is not all that different from the negotiations between nations.

There are also many skills that you learn in almost any job that will help you become a better student. Skills like time management, keeping a schedule, managing a budget, working in groups, computer skills, report writing, verbal communication, analyzing problems, being creative and meeting project deadlines are just a few skills that will help you no matter what your major.

Other relevant experiences include other activities in which you've been involved. This may include community work, church, PTA or anything else that you enjoy doing. It may also include hobbies and interests such as woodworking or crafting. In particular, you'll want to highlight any leadership roles that you've had or accomplishments you've made. For example, if you tutored math at your son's elementary school and are planning to return to college to get a degree in elementary education, then you'll definitely want to highlight that on your resume.

If you have been a stay at home mom or dad, be sure to list that as well. Don't be afraid to toot your own horn. It's a huge responsibility to manage a household and raise children. Detail the responsibilities that you are most proud of. You might also want to share what you did during your down time at home. Maybe you became a voracious reader, and this is part of why you want to go back to school. One student we met was a stay at home mom and started writing poetry during the (few and far between) quiet moments. She never thought much about it until we pointed out that having filled a journal with poetry and read the works of other poets was very impressive and should definitely be listed on her resume as well as in her application.

Depending on your own reasons for going back to school, you'll probably want to categorize your experiences in a way that makes the most sense. In general, put the most relevant and impressive items first. For example, let's say that you are planning to be a business major. You work in an office environment and also do volunteer work at a local battered women's shelter where one of your projects is to manage the volunteers who answer the hotlines. Instead of listing your job under "work experience" and the volunteer experience under "other experience," you may list them both under one category of "business experience." You could describe your volunteer work as having taught you about managing a team even if your team was a volunteer one. This makes it easy for the admission officers to see in one place all of your experience and skills that will help you be a better business major.

Admission resumes do not need to follow the strict formatting rules that employment resumes often do. You are trying to make life easy for the admission officers by showing them what is important. This means that you can create whatever categories you feel are necessary to accomplish this.

How To Match Your Resume To Your Goals

While your goal for writing a job resume may be to land a new job, your goal when writing a resume for college or graduate school admission is quite different. You want to demonstrate that you are academically prepared for the program and have experiences that will make you a strong student.

We've taken some common experiences and described them in a way that would illustrate their significance to a college admission officer. At the same time with only a page of space, we need to economize our words. While your experiences will be different than these examples, the important point is to study how we draw the connection whenever possible between the experience and the skills learned that would make you a better student.

UC Irvine. Completed 16 credit hours in required freshman courses. Received an "A" in Modern Psychology and achieved an overall GPA of 3.0.

GED. Successfully completed summer GED program while working full-time.

Macy's Sales Associate. Responsibilities included customer service and inventory. Named associate of the month for excellence in customer care.

Smith & Lewis, Marketing Associate. Responsible for working with team to develop marketing plans for clients. Conducted market research on location for new hotel and analyzed results of recent radio campaign for electronics store.

Library Volunteer. Dedicated five hours per week. Responsibilities included assisting the reference librarian with patron requests for information. Became proficient in using online databases to find information.

Crochet Workshop Leader. Taught a group of 35 students how to crochet. Class met twice a week over three months. Designed all lessons and exercises. All students graduated with basic knowledge of the craft.

Central High School PTA Secretary. Elected secretary responsible for attending all meetings, keeping accurate records of proceedings and participating in association activities.

Flower Arrangement. Self-taught flower arrangement through extensive study of books and by attending a workshop given by master arranger Sharon Kubota. Participated in annual flower arranging competitions.

Automotive repair. Self-taught mechanic able to completely overhaul an automobile engine.

```
Volunteered time to assist with York High
School Student Auto Club.
```

You can see that for each experience you want to highlight what is most impressive and give concrete examples of your level of skill whenever possible. Ideally, some of these things will also tie into what you plan to study. However, even if the connection is not obvious, college admission officers will understand and value your achievements. Knowing how to rebuild an engine may not be useful for a literature major, but the skills you acquired while learning how to do this are absolutely essential to being a successful student. College admission officers value all kinds of skills that will make you a good student from the obvious such as writing and math to the less obvious such as team work and time management.

SIX

How To Write
A Winning
Admission
Essay

How To Write A Winning Essay

In an ideal situation you would have the opportunity to sit down with each admission officer over a cup of coffee. With easy listening music in the background, you'd share with them what you've learned from your family, work and life in general as well as what your goals are for the future. On a relaxing afternoon and between bites of coffee cake, you and the admission officers would get to know each other better.

Unfortunately, as much as admission officers would like to do this, if they did they would never get through the thousands of applicants they have to review. So instead of a face-to-face, the admission officers provide you with the opportunity to write an admission essay. Sometimes called a personal statement or letter of intent, the essay is a way for you to share with the admission officers who you are beyond the facts and figures in your application.

Admission officers view the essay as an important window into who you are. Your grades and test scores, if applicable, give them an indication of your academic preparedness, and your application and resume give them the highlights of your accomplishments. But it is the essay in which you can delve into what motivates you and drives you to be who you are. It is the essay that will let them hear your voice, what makes you unique. Through the essay you can explain where you've been, where you are and where you'd like to go—and do so in your own words.

This is why colleges and graduate schools value the essay so highly. If you need to write an essay, it's vital that you spend the time to craft the strongest essay possible. It can literally make the difference between an acceptance and a rejection.

As an adult student, your approach to the essay will be much different than that of a high school senior. For high school seniors who are applying to colleges, the essay may be difficult because they aren't sure what to write about. Many high school students feel that they haven't had a life-changing or meaningful experience that has affected their life. One of the challenges that you may face is having too much to write about and too many of those experiences.

Finding The Perfect Topic

Before you start brainstorming topics, it's important to know what questions you will be asked. The best way to do this is to look at the applications of the schools that you are applying to and make a list of their questions. One of the most common complaints from admission officers is that applicants do not answer their questions in the essay. Don't fall into this trap. Tape the list of questions above your computer, on your bathroom mirror or on your refrigerator door to remind you of what you need to answer.

While questions differ by school, common questions include: What is an academic class that you've taken or project that you've done that has been meaningful? What do you do outside of the classroom? Why would you like to attend this institution? And the most common question of all, tell us about yourself.

You can see that colleges and graduate schools are trying to get at how prepared you are for the academic rigors, what you can bring to the institution and how the institution will meet your needs. The questions are purposefully broad to allow you to get at the heart of what is important to you. So while you can't necessarily choose to write about anything, you usually have flexibility to select how you answer the question and the approach that you take. The decision of what to write about can be difficult. Some students spend as much time thinking about what to write as they do actually writing.

As you begin to brainstorm topics, it's critical that you not write just what you think the colleges want to hear. A major complaint from admission officers is that students try to give what they think the admission officers want to read. Don't start second guessing what the admission officers want to read. If you try to filter your ideas by what you assume will impress the colleges, you'll severely limit your chances of coming up with a winning topic that is both original and a true reflection of you.

Start By Taking A Hard Look At Yourself

One of the best ways to jumpstart your brainstorming is to ask questions about yourself. Ask yourself about your goals—what your academic and career goals are and why. Reflect on your experiences—what meaningful ones you've had in school, work and elsewhere. Think about yourself—what motivates you, what values you have, how you have grown, what experiences or people have helped shape who you are.

Here is a list of specific questions that you should try answering if you find yourself facing writer's block:

- How have you excelled in your work?

- What tangible contributions have you made as an employee?

- How have you shown initiative?

- When and how do you work as part of a team?

- What is your biggest workplace success? Failure?

- What have you done at work or in other activities that you feel has prepared you to go back to college or graduate school?

- What qualities are most important to you in selecting a program?

- What made you decide to attend this particular school?

- What do you hope to get out of your education?

- How will you apply this knowledge to your future career plans?

- Why is it essential for you to go back to school at this point in your life?

- How will you personally enhance the campus community? What will you add?

- What makes you unique?

- What do you like to do outside of work? Why?

- Who is the most influential person in your life? What have you learned?

- What is the most difficult thing you have done? Why did you do it?

- What was the best and worst experience you've had at work and in your personal life?

By asking yourself these types of questions, you will be able to generate a list of your most meaningful influences, experiences and beliefs. This list will provide all of the examples and themes that you will use when answering the various essay questions.

At this point, don't rule out any answers. Don't think about what would make a good or poor essay. The idea is to allow your creativity to take over and to not be selective about what you write. Once you are tapped out, take a break. Go for a walk, or sleep on it. Come back a day or two later and see if you can add to your list.

Keep Asking Why

You could really cheat yourself when answering the above questions by simply writing down the obvious. If you answered the question of the most difficult thing that you have done by simply writing, "Climbing to the top of Mt. Kilimanjaro," you're only halfway done. You need to ask why. Why did you climb it? (Hopefully, not just because it was there.) Bring to bear the full strength of your analytical ability. Your essay is also a sample of your ability to think and analyze. Especially if it's been a long time since you were in school or if you did poorly in school in the past, it's very important that you show the admission officers that you are capable of deeply analyzing an issue.

So keep pushing yourself by asking why. Here is the thought process that should happen inside your head. Don't forget to take copious notes on your answers.

Q: What is the most difficult thing you have done?

A: Climb Mt. Kilimanjaro.

Q: Why did you climb it?

A: I enjoy challenges.

Q: Why specifically did you challenge yourself in this way?

A: I wanted to see if I would fail. I have a fear of failure and felt that if I was able to successfully make it to the summit I might have more self-confidence in other areas of my life.

Now you're getting somewhere and beginning to uncover significant and interesting thoughts. Keep pushing deeper until you can go no further. Do this for every topic idea. It's not easy and may take days to complete. (It may also give you a headache.) If you outline your topics in this manner, you will not only discover some truly unique aspects about yourself, but you may also find connections between ideas to answer one of your essay questions.

Eliminating Bad Topics

If you've taken the time to subject yourself to the intense brainstorming and self-reflection described above, you'll end up with several pages of potential topics. Not all of these are going to be winners. To help you narrow down your list, you need to see how each potential topic or idea will contribute to the overall message of your essay and application.

Through your application—and especially in your essays—you are creating a picture of yourself for the admission officers. Generally, you want to convey to the schools that you are prepared for the academic rigors, understand what being a student will involve, are motivated and willing to overcome the challenges and will contribute to the class and college community at large.

For each experience or idea that you have listed, think about the greater message it conveys, the underlying meaning it relates. It may be an example of a character trait, an important realization or simply something that gives you pleasure. Try to analyze each to uncover what messages you can draw out of each idea. A good essay is not just a well-written narrative. A good essay is an analysis and demonstrates your ability to take a step back and think critically about your experiences. You want to not only describe your experiences, but you want to explain the meaning of them.

You will discover that some ideas don't have a strong message or that they convey something that you don't necessarily want to share with an admission officer. Now is the time to cross out these ideas. Keep only those that will help you make your point. Refer back to your list of specific questions from the colleges. It should be taped to your bathroom mirror, remember? If your topics or ideas don't address the specific questions of the school, they should be eliminated.

Once you have your list of topics, the message that they convey and which questions they can answer, it's time to share. It will save you a lot of time and effort if you get some feedback before you start to write.

Talk It Out With A Friend

There's a reason why there is a thriving industry built around therapy. It actually helps to talk things through. This is especially true for essay writing. If you are stuck on a topic, not sure if it's a good one or just want make sure you've thought of everything, talk it out with a friend, family member or colleague.

Ask if it sounds like an interesting topic and if it coveys an important aspect of your background or personality. You will be surprised by how much discussing your ideas with someone—even before you've written a single word—can help.

If you share your ideas with more than one person, you may get conflicting responses. That's fine. At this stage you just want to explore the topic and get feedback. Often this feedback will help you dissect the potential of the topic, uncover new possibilities, alert you to possible problems and fine-tune your message. This will save you time when it comes to actually writing your essays.

So share your list of topics with anyone who will listen. Keep an open mind and listen to what they have to say. It will only help you write a stronger essay.

Look For A Snowflake

One key trait of a good essay topic is that like a snowflake, it should be one-of-a-kind. You don't want to write an essay that someone else could write. This can be hard to do since every applicant is answering the same questions. So with all of these potential similarities, how do you write an essay that is different? It goes back to your ability to analyze your experiences and to be self-reflective about what you have learned. Like the classic Kurosawa movie, *Rashomon*, where various witnesses describe the same crime, each interprets the same events differently.

Let's say that you are an avid rock climber. If you've carefully analyzed and reflected on why you enjoy climbing and what motivates you to scale a barren cliff every weekend, you will find that the reasons are as unique to you as your personality. Now you will probably have some shared reasons with other rock climbers. Since these are not unique, you can safely eliminate them from your list. While there is nothing wrong with acknowledging some of the more common themes, such as the joy of finding a route to the top of a rock wall, it should not be the central theme of your essay.

As you look at your list of topics, be cautious of the ones that are not unique. Ask yourself, "If I write about this, will I be the only one who can write this essay in this way?" If the answer is no, then you may need to rethink your approach.

Ultimately, you want your essays to be unique and original. But the good news is that if you analyze your topic deeply enough and you are genuine, it will be unique. It's when you don't push yourself far enough in your analysis or when you try to second-guess what the admission officers want to hear that you get into problems with originality.

Everyone has a snowflake like essay inside of them. You just need to work to discover it.

Take The Passion Test

Now that you have a shorter list of topics that you've thought about, shared with some friends and tested for originality, the last step is to apply the passion test. One of the best ways to get inspired when writing your essays is to write about something that inspires you. When you write about something that you are passionate about, the words will flow more fluidly and contain energy that the reader can actually feel jumping off the page.

The passion test is especially useful when you face the common dilemma of choosing between a topic that you think the admission officers will be impressed by and a topic that you are truly passionate about. For example, on a question about what you do in your spare time you might be tempted to write about how you play the stock market instead of your true love of macramé. You might think that stocks and bonds will be more impressive to an admission officer than weaving cords and beads into plant hangers. But if you're passionate about macramé and don't take any pleasure in investing, then if you try to write about investing you are going to have an essay that is uninspired and generic. But your essay on the delight you get from matching the right macramé fibers and beads to create the perfect plant hanger would be filled with passion and be much more interesting and memorable.

Admission officers have a sixth sense for detecting when you are catering to what you think you should write rather than being true to yourself. So if you have topics on your list that you are not passionate about, put a big "X" next to them. Focus on those ideas that you are excited about and that truly represent who you are. These will become the best essays because they come from the heart.

Time To Write

So you think you have a winning topic? Now the only thing left to do is to write. It's time to pull out that notebook or fire up the laptop and start putting words to the page. The ultimate test of whether or not your topic is a good one is to actually turn it into an essay.

As You Write, Don't Forget Detail. As you are writing, don't forget to give detail. Without going overboard, adding a few details helps to make a story come alive. For example, let's say that you are answering a question about your career goals. You could answer this question by stating that your goal is to become a high school teacher and explaining the value of education. This would be a passable essay.

A better essay, however, would explain the past experiences that you've had that have inspired you to want to teach. You could describe how you volunteered at your child's school and took part in helping the children learn to read. Then, you could write about what made you decide that now is the right time to return to school and how your education will enable you to meet your goal. Lastly, you could convey what you hope to achieve as a teacher and what will motivate you in the future.

By including such details, you'll create a compelling story that the admission officers can relate to and will remember. It will help to make your essay unique and share with them some important aspects of who you are.

Share Yourself. Speaking of the importance of sharing who you are, a common mistake that many students make when writing is that they forget that they are the subjects of the essay. You must remember that the essay is about you. It sounds easy enough, but many students write so much about an influential person or event that they forget to explain the effect that this influential person or event has had on them. Let's look at an example.

Schools will frequently ask why you want to attend their institution. They ask this as a way of making sure that there is a fit between your goals and what their school has to offer. The first thing that most applicants do is pull out the school's brochure or click over to its website and start summarizing information about the school. They list the courses that are offered, the resources for adult students or the alumni services.

When answering this kind of question, it's important to conduct research about the school to be able to answer why you want to attend an institution. The mistake that most students make is that this is all they write about. The important second step that they are missing is to show how the features of the schools match their goals. In other words, a mediocre essay will provide a list of interesting courses offered by a school. A better one shows why the applicant is interested in those classes and how they will apply to his or her future.

It's important to bring yourself into any question that is asked. When writing about an influential person, don't just give a biography of that person. Explain how that person has helped shape who you are. When writing about an academic experience that you've had, don't just write about the experience itself. Share what you gained from the experience and how it has helped you to develop your academic growth. The key is that no matter what the topic is, you need to keep yourself in the essay.

Edit And Re-edit

Don't expect that as you are writing your essay that your first draft will be perfect. There are very few writers, if any, who can produce their best writing in one pass. Your essay will be stronger if you spend time editing it and even spend time away from it.

Fortunately, you don't have to go through the editing process alone. It helps to have others provide assistance. Ask your spouse, coworker, employer or friend to read over your essay. There are two types of editors that you need.

First, you need editors who can comment on the content and writing of your essay. They should let you know if it conveys who you are, if you've left something significant out and if it sounds like you. Ask them also about the writing style, your word choice and the flow of the essay. It can be difficult editing your own work by yourself because you are so close to it. By getting others to give you feedback, you may get a fresh perspective or new idea.

Second, you need editors who will proofread your work. You may find an editor who can provide feedback on both content and proofreading, but you may need to ask two different people. Ask your proofreading editor to look for grammatical, spelling and other technical errors right before you submit your work.

It also helps to spend time away from your writing. Stop writing for a day or two and then return to your work. You will approach your work with a fresh eye, and it is amazing how you can shed writer's block this way.

Recycling

If you think about the number of schools that you are applying to and then think that each school may require one to three essays, you are in for a lot of writing! You may have several essays to write. The good news is that you can recycle some of your essays. In other words, you can modify an essay that you've written for one school to apply to another school.

For example, let's say one school asks you to write an essay about a person who is important to you and another school asks you to write about one of your values. If you wrote about how your mother taught you to be optimistic, you could use this essay to answer both questions. Writing about your mother would answer the question of a person who is important to you, and optimism would provide one of your values.

If you decide to recycle your essays, make sure that you modify the introduction, conclusion and other areas that are necessary to make the essay fit the new question. You may be able to use the original essay with few changes or just a small portion of the original essay.

One thing to remember though is that you don't want to go overboard recycling. Ultimately, your essay needs to answer the question asked so you don't want to stretch an essay to try to fit a question that it just doesn't fit. If anything, it will make your answer seem off-kilter.

The last thing you want to do is make sure that you have the correct name of the school in the essay. Almost every school in the country receives an essay each year with the wrong name in it. That's not the impression that you want to leave.

The 18 Most Common Essay-Writing Mistakes

In the next chapter you will read examples of essays. Before you do, however, we want to share with you the 18 most common essay-writing mistakes. These are mistakes that students commit every year and that have a disastrous effect on their chances of getting admitted. Learn from their mistakes so you don't commit any of these errors in your own essays.

So without further ado, we present to you our list of the 18 most common essay-writing mistakes:

1. Not answering the question.

It may seem like an obvious mistake, but many applicants don't answer the question. Or they answer part of the question but not all of it. If you are asked about a time that you've been a leader and the impact that your leadership had, don't just describe when you have been a leader. Make sure that you also address the impact of your leadership. This is a mistake that many students make when recycling their essays or using the same essay for more than one school. If you do recycle your essays, edit them carefully to make sure that they completely answer the question asked.

2. Showing that you know nothing about the school.

Colleges and graduate schools take pride in the fact that they each have their own strengths. They want to see you address those strengths and how you will benefit from them. While it can be tempting to copy and paste your essays from one school to another, you'll want to instead make sure that each essay addresses the strengths of each school. Admission officers can tell when your essays are so general that you have used them to apply to multiple schools or haven't done your homework about the strengths of their program. In at least one of your essays, be sure you show how the school's particular strengths match your needs.

3. Parroting back what's on the website or brochure.

To try to show their knowledge about a particular school, some applicants go to the school's website or brochure and copy text from them into their essays. Admission officers are oftentimes the ones who write this material, and it does not impress them to see their own descriptions of their schools in essays. You need to do your own research. Visiting a school or at least talking to some of its students and faculty by telephone is critical. By doing so you can include in your essays what you have learned from sitting in on classes, interacting with students or observing an activity. This kind of insight demonstrates that you have taken the time to research the school and understand what it has to offer you.

4. Assuming the persona of who you think the school wants.

Some applicants try to be who they think the admission officers want them to be. They exaggerate strengths that they think will impress the school or even try to flatter the admission officers by declaring that their school is the only one for them. Unless you mean it, the admission officers will see through this hyperbole. It is better to reveal your honest intentions, strengths and opinions. You will produce more genuine and believable essays that will ultimately help you get admitted.

5. Not revealing enough about you.

The questions you answer may be about your family, a figure you'd like to have dinner with or travel you've done. But the bottom line is that the admission officers ask these questions as a way to learn about you. So instead of writing an autobiography of a historical figure or a detailed travelogue of the places you've been, make sure the focus is still on you. If you were writing about a historical figure you might write about what you would want to learn from him or her and why this is important to you. If you were writing about travel, you would want to spend time on how it has affected you versus your daily itinerary. In other words, regardless of the question, remember that the essay is still about you.

6. Trying to be funny when you're not.

It takes a very skilled writer to write a humorous essay. If you're not this type of writer, your essay is not the place to try to be. You can't miraculously change your writing style overnight. Often your attempt at humor may appear trite or plain silly. It's better to stick to your own style.

7. Not knowing why you want to go back to school.

As you answer the questions, you will need to explain why you want to go back to school. The more you understand your motivations, the stronger your essays will be. You don't need to have every step of your future career worked out because admission officers understand that a college or graduate degree will help you figure this out. But you do need to have some good reasons about why you want a degree at this point in your life.

8. Forgetting to tie in your goals with the school.

It's important that you not only explain your career goals but also elaborate on how the school will help you to achieve these goals. Admission officers want to see this connection. This helps them to see what you will gain from attending their school.

9. Not writing about individual achievements.

While it's important to show that you can be a team player, it is also important to define your individual accomplishments. Some students only write about their accomplishments as a part of a team but never address what they contributed as an individual. This is a big mistake. If you are writing about a group accomplishment, make sure to describe how you individually contributed to the success of the group.

10. Writing a resume in paragraph form.

Your essays should be more than glorified resumes. In other words, don't just list your accomplishments. Describe the importance of them and what you have gained from the experiences. Analyze and reflect on their value.

11. Not explaining what you have learned.

More important than your actual accomplishments is what you have gained from them. This is the key piece of information that admission officers want to know. As you're writing your essays, think about what you have gotten out of the experience, how you would approach a similar situation differently and how you have applied your knowledge to other interactions.

12. Running out of time.

It is a mistake to think that you can develop meaningful essays overnight. Thinking about your goals, the meaning of a college or graduate school education and your life's accomplishments takes a lot of quality time. Give yourself enough time to think about what you've done and what you believe in to develop the strongest essays possible.

13. Not having a point.

As you are writing your essays, it's not enough for the essays to be well written and tell a good story. They also need to convey a message to the admission officers. In other words, what strengths do they reveal? How do they portray you? What impression do they leave? Try to take a step back to examine the message that you are sharing with the reader through your essay. If you can't find it, then your essay is probably lacking in focus.

14. Weak introspection or analysis.

Admission officers don't just want to know about your actions. They want to get inside of your head to understand your thoughts

and motivations. Try to share what you are thinking to give them a better idea of who you are. Admission officers expect to see both self-reflection and analysis in your essays.

15. Skimping on editors.

It's difficult to edit your own essays when you are so close to the material. One of the best ways to improve your work is by having someone else give you feedback. Find colleagues, friends and family members who are strong writers to look at your work. Ask them to point out weaknesses, to check for continuity and to make suggestions on how to strengthen your messages. Their feedback is a necessity to write a successful essay.

16. Losing your voice through the editing process.

While it is critical that you get feedback from editors, it is equally important that you use the feedback as a guideline for your writing but that you still retain your own voice. You don't want your work so heavily edited that it no longer sounds like you. Similarly, if you blindly accept everyone's suggestions you might end up with an essay written by committee rather than by you. Editing should enhance your writing, not take the place of it.

17. Not proofreading.

Almost every admission officer can point to an essay each year in which an applicant writes the wrong school's name. A little proofreading can go a long way. It's not enough to use your computer's spell check. Take the time to read each word of your essays and check grammar, punctuation and spelling. Or if you aren't skilled in copyediting, find someone who is.

18. Not taking some time away from your writing.

Like a fine Napa wine, essays take time to develop. Often the best way to improve your essays is to take a break from writing them. So write your essays and then allow yourself some time away. When you return to look at them you'll have a fresh perspective and will be able to see how you can improve them.

These are the most common essay-writing mistakes. Keep these in mind as you write your own masterpiece. Simply by avoiding these mistakes you can save yourself a lot of unnecessary aggravation, and you will insure that you have the strongest essay possible.

Successful Admission Essays

Successful Admission Essays

When you first learned to drive, it was one thing to sit in driver's education class to learn the theory of driving, but it was another thing entirely to sit behind the wheel and actually drive. Like learning to drive, essay writing is best learned by experience. The purpose of this chapter is to provide you with examples of essays that other successful adult students have written.

From reading these essays, you'll see that there is no absolute "right" or "wrong" way to write an essay. In fact, there are an unlimited number of topics to write about and ways to approach the essay. And contrary to popular belief, you don't have to be a professional writer to write a great essay.

In the following pages you'll meet students just like you. Some of them never attended college, some of them spent some years in school and some of them are pursuing graduate degrees. They are parents, part-time and full-time employees and senior citizens.

What we hope you'll learn from these essays is that to write the strongest essay possible, you just need to be you. Present where you are and what you'd like to achieve by furthering your education. This is what these students did, and they are all well on their way to their goals.

Important note: Please remember that these essays are only examples of ways that some students have successfully written their admission essays. Your essays will naturally be your own.

Explaining A Break In Your Education

Dana R.
Columbia University

Dana left her native Israel at the age of 16 to be reunited with her father in the United States. She immersed herself into American high schools, first in Miami and then in Charlotte, North Carolina. Although

Dana always planned on going to college, she had to return to Israel first to serve a mandatory 18-month term for female soldiers as required by Israeli citizenship. She excelled in the military and served for three years, finishing her service as a first lieutenant.

Dana's plans were to return to the U.S. to attend college, but little did she know, life was about to throw her a curve ball. Her father had returned to Israel, was in poor health and was unable to find work. So they reversed roles. For a year and a half, Dana remained in Israel to support her father, first from her military wages and later as a restaurant manager.

Four years ago, Dana was able to return to the U.S., but first another hurdle presented itself. She was diagnosed with a bladder tumor and didn't have health insurance. She managed to receive an operation and is now tumor-free but faces substantial debt due to paying for the medical expenses without insurance.

Finally, Dana found her way to Columbia University, where she is pursuing a bachelor's degree. Eventually, she hopes to attend law school to become a criminal defense attorney.

Dana's Essay

Many people I met over the years said that I would most likely change my mind plenty of times about my school of choice. I was a 12-year-old girl living in a small suburb of Tel Aviv when I decided to go to college and eventually law school in New York. At the time, the decision seemed like a fantasy to my peers and teachers. After all, I lived more than 10 years and 7,000 miles away from my dreams. I would mature and inevitably change my mind they said. Thirteen years passed and practically every aspect of my life indeed has changed, except for my determination to achieve my goal of attending Columbia University. Ironically, I arrived in the United States even sooner than I expected.

I left Israel at the age of 16. The tension between my mother and me exceeded the average teenage hormonal-related explosions, and we decided that for the sake of our mutual sanity it would be best if I reunite with my father in the United States. It was not an easy decision. Leaving my friends, my secure social circle, my familiar culture and my school at such a crucial age of emotional development were just a few reasons for hesitancy. I had to be ready to subject myself to a struggle that involved beginning a new life in a foreign land, a new school and a foreign language to replace my native Hebrew. My decision-making process was calculated but not lengthy, and I arrived in Miami within a month.

My acceptance into the Miami school system was not exactly what I expected. I thought the registration in the new school would include a close examination into my academic past in Israel and an assessment of my level of English. Instead, I was placed in typical tenth grade classes and not surprisingly, miserably failed my first semester. I failed most classes, however, not because I was unfamiliar with the material but because I struggled with the English language. Learning different subjects in a foreign language was an art I had yet to master. The system thoroughly confused me, as I did not know the meaning or significance of a GPA or class rank nor did I know that my achievements in my sophomore year in high school had a direct effect on determining them. With time, however, I learned the ways of the system and made great progress in learning the English language. Just when it seemed I had adapted to my new surroundings, my father decided to leave Miami, and we relocated to Charlotte, North Carolina, in the fall.

I was ecstatic in Charlotte. The school I attended requested the translation of my Israeli academic history. I excelled in all of my classes; I understood how to utilize the system to my benefit with Advanced Placement classes and extracurricular activities and, most importantly, I enjoyed it. I faced another obstacle when my father was unable to find work in Charlotte and decided to return to Israel. If I left with him, it would have meant disrupting my education flow again, so I decided to stay. Although my father's departure was very difficult for me, as I stayed in Charlotte alone at the age of 17, I do not think I could have made a better decision. I was eager to learn and excel in my studies. The combination of my appetite for knowledge and my teachers' desire to impart it concluded in a highly satisfying senior year. My studies, the sciences and humanities alike, fascinated me. I was ready for college after graduation, but it was time to return to Israel to fulfill my duty of required military service.

The mandatory military service in Israel dictates an 18-month term for female soldiers, and I commenced my service shortly after my return in August 1996. Boot camp, physical training, uniform, drill sergeant, mess hall and the like become an Israeli soldier's main word bank almost overnight. Another instantaneous change comes with the burden as well as danger of wearing the uniform. I was a soldier in Israel during a period in which kidnapping soldiers was the modus operandi of terrorism, and wearing the uniform meant turning into a moving target. After a month in boot camp, I was recruited to the Navy and stationed in its southern most base in Eilat. Shortly afterwards, navy headquarters notified me of my eligibility to begin evaluation and testing for officers' training. My eligibility was based upon the preliminary intelligence and psychological tests. Since officers' training is voluntary, I could have declined the offer, but I was very enthusiastic about serving my country, and the opportunity assured a longer term in the navy and a more influential position. Following rigorous training, I received the rank of second lieutenant in June 1997. I was then stationed in the Israeli Naval Commando Unit where I earned the rank of first lieutenant and where I stayed until the end of my military service of two and a half years in February 1999. I was proud to be an officer in the Israeli Defense Forces, and I felt lucky to have even an iota of the country's defense responsibility on my shoulders. At the conclusion of my service, although I was ready to move back to the United States and resume my discontinued education, financial troubles in the family commanded a different reality.

My father had not found work in Israel. Failing health and his age closed many doors for him. Since the rest of his family isolated themselves from him, he had no one to turn to but me. Therefore, we reversed roles. In 1997, when I was 19, I began supporting my father, first with my modest military salary and later with my earnings as a restaurant bartender and manager. Since my mother did not support me and I was financially independent, I could not leave Israel. I had to postpone my plans for an additional year and a half, to save for my move to the United States and to leave my father with something to live on until I settled in New York. Some consider my actions a great sacrifice. I, however, consider it my responsibility, an obligation to my father that I am happy to be able to fulfill. I was patient, and I finally returned to the United States in the summer of 2000.

Coming to New York was the first step I took toward realizing my dream of studying at Columbia University. After six months of apartment hunting and a nearly endless job search, I settled in the northern corner of Harlem and found steady employment in Manhattan. Just when everything seemed to be working out for me, I was surprised by another impediment. At the end of February 2001, I rushed to the emergency room with a condition the doctors later diagnosed as a developed bladder tumor. Without health insurance, I was at the mercy of two surgeons who slipped me into the hospital the following week for surgery. The operation was successful; I was tumor free although in considerable debt from the costly medical procedures. After finding a health insurance plan that would enable me to return for periodic check-ups, paying my hospital debt, managing my everyday needs and assisting my father, I was back at square one. I had to ensure my well being before making the commitment to return to school, and I have never felt more ready than I do today.

My goal is to complete my bachelor's degree at Columbia University's School of General Studies and then continue my education at Columbia's School of Law. I am in awe of the United States Constitution, and I wish to be able to practice in its support one day. The years of delaying my education have only enhanced my desire to return to the classroom. I know I would surely be here seeking college admission to Columbia University regardless of my decision to leave Israel when I was 16. I strongly believe, however, that the years of studying in the United States, serving in the Israeli Defense Forces and working to support my father and myself have equipped me with the necessary strength, discipline and resolve to achieve my goals. Without those years I would undoubtedly still be here, but I would lack all the priceless experiences and lessons gained through my journeys.

Juanjuan Blout
Wellesley College

Juanjuan Blout grew up in Jiangsu Province in southeast China where the means of survival was rice paddies. She was always an academic-minded child and was affectionately known as the "little girl who almost burned the whole hut because she wouldn't put down a book even when she was shoving hay into the stove." When her college dreams eluded her, she attended a free vocational school that trained her to be a middle school English teacher, which she did for three years.

Four years ago, Juanjuan decided to take her life in a new direction and immigrated to the United States. She began her college education at the University of Massachusetts-Boston before attending Wellesley College, where is now an Elisabeth Kaiser Davis Scholar.

Applying to college as not only an adult student but also as a foreign student presented unique challenges for Juanjujan. She felt disadvantaged because she did not have the strongest SAT scores, studied under a different academic system and began speaking English only 10 years ago.

She asked herself, "Will the admission office appreciate my life experience? Will I be able to handle the academic requirements since I am going to study in my second language?"

But in the end, Juanjuan believes her experience living in China helped her college application. She says, "All I had was the strength accumulated through the years I lived as a working adult in China. Remember your life experience is a valuable component of you as an individual."

Juanjuan's Essay

I came from a tiny village in southeast China where people rely solely on the rice paddies for a living. I started to plant rice shoots with the company of numerous mosquitoes when I was 10. Having never been to school, my parents know the hardships in life as the lowest-level members of society. There are no accurate words to describe how much they struggled in order to put me through high school, simply by bending their backs and working bare-footed on the paddies from dawn to dusk. I was known as "the little girl who almost burned the whole hut because she wouldn't put down the book even when she was shoving hays to the stove." I didn't let them down. My childhood was spent in our small hut made out of mud and straw, where there was nothing much except a wooden bed for my parents, my sister and me, a lime stove in the corner and a wall full of certificates addressed to me from my school, the only thing that my parents were proud of.

I studied various subjects in high school: math, physics, chemistry, geography and history. Though I had the best academic performance in the class and very possibly would become the first college student in the village, in the summer 13 years ago when it was the time for me to choose colleges, my parents just couldn't do anything more to help but sigh. Given the fact that there wasn't any financial aid system available in China at that time, I accepted my fate and gave up any hope for a college education. I was only 17 years old then. In desperation, I attended a vocational school that would train me to become a middle school teacher for a remote area in exchange for free tuition.

Thus I became a middle school English teacher when I turned 19 and stayed at that position for three years. It was a state-secured position that was considered dream-like for my parents, since I would be guaranteed a salary and shelter as long as I stayed. It was the most difficult decision I had to make in life when I resigned and went to southern China alone to pursue my passions. In the following five years, in an economic-open area that was relatively developed compared to the rest of China, I struggled for food and shelter. I remember the Saturday afternoon when outside the Red Cross blood station I debated whether I should sell my blood for my next meal, the evenings when I crawled onto a piece of newspaper under the wooden bench on the cross-country train, the nights when I fought with the fleas in my bed and the dawn I fled the mafia-owned factory to gamble my future…until five years ago when I owned my own import agency in the city of Xiamen and life started to smile on me.

Four years ago I immigrated to the U.S. Facing a new society and new opportunities, I wanted nothing more than to become a college student, and I knew this was the right path for me if I ever wanted to find a foothold here. I love the feeling of sitting in classrooms and listening to professors. The joy from knowing that I am learning and I am developing myself lured me like a fragrance. Luckily, with the financial support from my husband's family, the University of Massachusetts-Boston accepted me. Thus, 10 years after my graduation from high school, my dream of college came true.

Goals For Your Education

Nancy Hutton
Mount Holyoke College

Nancy Sue Hutton had a brief college stint after high school but left and pursued a successful career in publishing. She became the director of sales and marketing at a publishing company, but she was denied a well-deserved promotion because she didn't have a college degree. It was then that Nancy decided to earn her degree no matter what. At first she attended community college courses via the Internet to accommodate her work schedule.

She later applied to Mount Holyoke College to a program for older re-entry students. She says, "That made a huge difference. I felt that there was going to be a certain accommodation for my past but that I would still be held to the same high standards as their other, traditionally-aged students."

When she applied to Mount Holyoke College, she tried to convey to the admission office her academic passion and what she wanted to achieve. She says, "The college would rather have someone who has a plan and changes her mind later than someone who is ambivalent and unfocused."

Nancy is currently studying for a master's of theological studies at Harvard Divinity School. Why study religion? "Religion is one of many lenses available for viewing the human experience and how people create meaning in their lives," she says, adding, "I think that religion is unique because it is nearly universal, has historical evidence that is among the oldest remnants available and provides one of the few windows on women's contributions."

After Harvard, Nancy plans to pursue a Ph.D. and teach at the college level one day. But she doesn't want to limit herself to teaching. "I want to use the lessons that I've learned to act and be an activist in community efforts fostering harmony, peace and coalition building," she says.

Nancy's Essay

I have a successful and rewarding career working for a publishing company whose books help people learn. For me, that has been about as close to "right livelihood" as I have ever enjoyed. My children are grown with families of their own a few hours away. I live in the country with deer and wild turkeys as neighbors. The ocean is a short drive away. What more could I want?

When I went back to college last year, it was for the purpose of freshening my business skills. My plan was to get an undergraduate degree in business then proceed to an MBA. Along the way, something unexpected happened. While studying Western Civilization-Ancient World (History 4A), I was struck by the role of women throughout ancient history. What happened that made women's roles so subservient? I was sufficiently intrigued to follow that up with Western Civilization-to the 1800's (History 4B) AND Philosophy-Comparative Western Religion (PHIL 25). I discovered that some scholars claim that during the Inquisitions and European Witch Hunts, 9 million women were killed. While the number is in dispute, it is agreed that this was the largest non-war-related murder of a people BY THEIR OWN in recorded history. Wow! And that was just ONE compelling insight that got me stirred up. (You did ask me to be brief!)

I couldn't put the topic down. And the topic wouldn't let me put it down. It seemed that around every corner I was finding books or articles that continued to stimulate more questions. So many questions and so little time! I work between 40 and 50 hours a week with extensive travel. I was sufficiently challenged taking two college classes over the Internet. I just couldn't seem to find extra time to explore these issues as fully as I wanted to. It was becoming evident that it mattered more to me to ask the questions and look for the answers than maintain my employment. One day while clicking through screens on a completely unrelated topic (as if there are "accidents"), there was a small banner ad about girl's education. To this day, I have no idea why I felt compelled to click on that small, obscure ad. I don't even remember the specifics of the ad, something about supporting educational options for girls. My eye caught the fine print at the bottom, "Sponsored by the National Ad Council" (or whomever) and "Mount Holyoke College." I clicked on the MHC link and my life changed.

That night I read virtually every page on the website. I read the course descriptions, read about the dormitories, read what they were having for breakfast next week. I read about the professors, about the facilities and of course, about the Frances Perkins Program. And then, just to make sure, I opened the site map and checked that I hadn't missed anything. Here was a community of smart women engaged in exploring the world in a way that I keenly wanted to be part of. And there was a special program for older re-entry students. Not just a program but a real community of older students. I looked at their pictures and read their stories. They were like I was! It sounded too good to be true! When I read the descriptions for major studies for women's studies (i.e., "provokes questions, discussions, disagreements and illuminating insights") and critical social thought, I knew in my heart that this was where I was supposed to be. Here I could explore the questions that have made me restless and hopefully find some answers that would be relevant. And do it in a community-based context that would be a valuable part of the process (I appreciated that 98 percent of the students lived on-campus.)

I've got to tell you that just because I got the wake-up call, I didn't immediately respond with, "Okay, let's go!" I struggled with fear and self-doubt and denial. But the call didn't go away. Rather, I found myself at work, while on hold, clicking back to the MHC website for just another peek. Even though only a week had passed since the first click on the MHC website, it was now or never. The deadline for application was only weeks away. I sent for the application for admission.

Now I have gratefully accepted the gift of the call. It's what I have to do. It's what I choose to do. What a treat to have something in my life that makes me feel so engaged, so passionate, so alive! It is so important that I will give up my security; I will give up my possessions (yet another prospective tag-sale about to be in progress!); I will give up my current way of being to plunge into this Sea of Uncertainty. Is the water cold? I don't know. Where will I end up? I don't know. For now, I'm secure in the belief that it's the journey, not the destination. I've always known what I need to know, when I need to know it. And so here I am. I am knocking on your door and asking you to invite me to join you.

Huan Hsu
George Mason University

Huan Hsu had one of the few Chinese faces growing up in a predominantly Mormon town in Utah. Right after high school, he attended the College of William and Mary in Williamsburg, Virginia, majoring in psychology and biology.

It was 1999 and "tech was still king," so Huan took a job in San Francisco with a high-tech public relations firm. "It was a nice first job, terribly lucrative but also pretty unsatisfying," he says. "Pitching journalists and writing press releases wasn't the best way to stretch my creative impulses."

In the summer of 2000, Huan quit and worked at a summer camp in New Hampshire to take time to figure out what to do next. Boston was his next stop. For the next two years, he coached a college tennis team but felt like he wasn't "using his brain much." To satisfy his intellectual curiosity, he took a continuing education writing workshop, which "rekindled an old but dormant love for writing."

Applying to graduate school was Huan's next step, but he wanted a back-up plan. So he pursued two career options with equal vigor: writing and the law. Huan was accepted into both laws schools and MFA programs, but ultimately, he decided to pursue writing. "I wanted to get an MFA because I thought it would be a great opportunity to focus all of my energy on reading and writing in a community of people who were just like me—suffering from an inexplicable desire to write," he explains. If he did go to law school, Huan says he would have always wondered what would have happened if he had pursued writing instead. He is now attending George Mason University in Fairfax, Virginia, for an MFA in creative writing with an emphasis in nonfiction writing.

Huan's Essay

My favorite toys while growing up were Legos. Stored in old cardboard ice cream tubs, I would dump them out each playtime onto a thin quilted blanket, orange on one side and purple paisley on the other (always placed orange side up, to see the pieces more easily). Sometimes my creations were planned; other times I would simply start with whatever caught my eye, shiny plastic pieces clinking in steady waves as I pawed through the pile. I would usually become so engrossed with my creation, feverishly working to bring my vision to life long after my friends or brother had lost interest, that my mother would literally have to shake me back to her world.

It would be easy to say that as I outgrew my Legos, writing became the way I satisfied my desire to create. Eventually, yes, but the self-consciousness that came with growing up Asian and non-Mormon in Utah made it hard to chase my muse. While my childhood was comfortable, it was also peppered with subtle reminders of my individuality—my parents jabbering in Chinese while shopping, categorical mispronunciations of my name, the only Hsu in classes full of Youngs and Hansens, confusing house calls from missionaries despite going to church every Sunday (not the right one, according to them). In my ethnicity I found nothing to appreciate, nothing to glorify, only embarrassment. While other boys my age wondered if it was okay to not make the basketball team, I wondered if it was okay to be Chinese.

By the time I arrived at college, the self-consciousness had melted away, replaced by an appreciation for and desire to understand different perspectives. Perhaps this ability to view the world through another's eyes is native to children of immigrants, to compensate for all those squirmy moments of wondering if and where we belong. Over the next four years, I tested the creative writing waters, fascinated by the thrilling gestalt of combining simple pieces into vessels that convey ideas, elicit feelings and generate thought.

After graduating, I spent the summer as a camp counselor in New Hampshire, then went back to Salt Lake and coached my old high school tennis team while I looked for a real job. A public relations agency in San Francisco extended an offer and I quickly accepted, excited to live in the city where I was born.

I spent the next year in California, growing fat on a bloated salary (we specialized in high-tech companies). It was a comfortable existence, but once I had experienced power lunches, weekly dry cleaning and accrued vacation days, I realized how little those things satisfied me intellectually, creatively and altruistically. For the past year I have been supervising junior tennis in New England with the United States Tennis Association, while also coaching the UMass-Boston men's varsity team.

Almost every recent graduate I've spoken with has said the hardest thing about leaving college is dealing with all the choices. Our lives go from perfectly measured simplicity to a confusing blizzard of possibilities. It can be enough to shellshock even the most prepared.

Is this the right thing to do? Will I regret this later? What do I really want, and where am I going?

These were the questions I asked myself when I was getting up at 5 a.m. to wait at the bus stop in the middle of Boston's cold, cold winter, brutal even to a mountain boy like me. I tried to trace the decisions that had put me there, scrounging for bus fare, trying to get by on a pair of jobs that didn't require a high school diploma and collectively paid me half of what I enjoyed in San Francisco. In Boston, I would typically return home 14 hours after leaving, with just enough time for a quick run, dinner and a bit of writing before falling asleep and doing it all over again.

Things eventually improved. I received a promotion, UMass went on to its best season in 11 years and though my days were still filled to the brim, I made time to take another creative writing workshop. While satisfying the impulses that had driven me to those college writing courses, it also provided the structure and direction necessary to develop nascent thoughts and shape loosely tied scribbles into sustained pieces, something that did not escape my notice.

Reflecting back on these experiences as I formed my final decision to pursue graduate study, I worried that perhaps my interest in an MFA degree was simply part of some quarter-life crisis, me searching for meaning in new cities and vocations the way 40-somethings buy Porsches. What I found over the next months was that I wanted the opportunity to turn on my brain again, that the breadth of my experiences not only provides fodder for my work but has also prepared me to give this undertaking the devotion it requires and deserves.

The more I have learned about MFA programs, the more eager I have become. Spend the next two years writing, learning, rubbing elbows with students and professors of surpassing ability and earn academic credit, too? What's the catch? In all seriousness, I know it is not that simple. I know I will probably run the gamut of emotions during my stay and may wonder what I've gotten myself into. I know that while no one aspires to be a struggling creative writer, financial success is not a given. I also know that the quiet, nagging urge to write has matured into a full-blown compulsion to immerse myself completely in the craft.

This past holiday season, I visited the FAO Schwartz on New York's Fifth Avenue. To my dismay, I found that today's Legos bear little resemblance to the ones with which I spent my afternoons. The pieces are larger, more specialized, their outcomes much more linear. I leave the store nostalgic, but comforted by the thought that writing is the Lego set I now carry with me, supplying the bricks that still lead to countless possibilities and infinite forms. I take it wherever I go, and every new experience, observation and reflection adds a piece to the pile or illuminates another function for an existing one. Sometimes I know right away exactly how I will use that piece; other times it washes in with the tide over and over before I realize what it can do and where it can go. I want to see how I can fit them all together. I want to pour out everything I have and get lost again, exploring new layers of the worlds I know and have yet to discover, trying out ideas I've only dreamed of trying. I want to sit back down on that orange blanket and make things until I run out of pieces.

Amy Olson
University of Wyoming

When Amy Olson was notified that her office in Fargo, North Dakota, was going to be closed, she took it as a sign to change careers. Amy had been working as an occupational safety trainer but had gone as far as she could and was already exploring other options. "I had nothing to lose and everything to win," she says.

After careful introspection, Amy decided that she wanted to become a psychologist. Because her undergraduate degree from the University of North Dakota was in biology, an unrelated field, this endeavor was a significant undertaking. She basically had to start the psychology career path from scratch in order to apply for Ph.D. programs in clinical psychology. For three semesters, she took undergraduate psychology courses to meet the prerequisites for applying to doctoral programs.

Amy applied to eight clinical psychology programs and entered the University of Wyoming's program in the fall of 2002. She chose the program for its atmosphere. She says, "Some programs are so cutthroat and competitive. Here, they really want everyone to do well."

Her department helps with the financial aspect of attaining the degree as well. Amy has a full tuition waiver and earns approximately $10,000 per year with a graduate assistantship, which covers her basic living expenses.

After graduate school Amy would like to work in a clinical setting and spend time researching trauma, bereavement and post-traumatic stress issues. She is also considering teaching on the side. By 2007, Amy expects to finish her Ph.D., and her dreams will be within reach.

Amy's Essay

The research on the impact of childhood maltreatment on relationships in adulthood, in combination with the commitment of the University of Wyoming Clinical Psychology Program to the scientist-practitioner model present the ideal environment for the combined expansion and application of knowledge, development of skills and utilization of my talents. This program will enable me to meet personal and professional goals, in addition to contributing to the advancement of psychology as a science.

While pursuing a biology degree, I was able to feed my curiosity, to learn how to methodically investigate the how, why and what if of science. My research investigated large theoretical questions and mechanisms. How does alcohol affect perception of depth? How is gender determined in various reptilian species? What effect does nicotine have on memory? I found the scientific process intriguing and rewarding. However, I continued to ask questions. How would this knowledge be applied? How would our actions benefit the populations with whom we were working? How would their day-to-day existence be affected?

My need to witness the impact on the community led to a program in occupational safety and environmental health. I was able to use my knowledge of biology and chemistry in an industrial setting, within the framework of federal regulations. One cornerstone of any safety program is the dissemination of information. I excelled at and enjoyed being a trainer. The information I was sharing and the programs and systems I was helping others to develop could be used to improve working conditions and to prevent injury and illness, at home or on the job. Another cornerstone of a successful safety program is the ability to motivate. A safety professional needs to motivate workers to perform their jobs in a safe manner. One needs to motivate upper management to commit resources to the program. A safety professional also must work to motivate the organization to create and perpetuate a safety culture. Colleagues would often express frustration and generalized feelings of stress as we discussed facing these challenges on a daily basis. This common theme was often accompanied by reports of illness, aches and pains. They were trying to motivate themselves to do their jobs and to motivate others. In the meantime, physically, they felt terrible. The stress people were experiencing and voicing was manifesting itself physically. Often, people recognized the pattern but were unable, unwilling or unsure of how to go about changing it. Again, I asked questions. How? Why? What if? I wanted to look into the mind-body interaction more closely. While applying my knowledge and experience, I had gotten away from the scientific process.

I took the opportunity to reassess my professional goals in terms of my personal goals. I had seen the effects of stress and trauma on people's lives. I had seen people striving to create a sense of balance for themselves. The science and issues I wanted to delve into more deeply fall under the heading of psychology. The undergraduate courses I took, not because they were required, but because I enjoyed them, were my psychology courses. Questions that interest me include: What are the life-long ramifications of early trauma?

My life experiences have brought me into contact with individuals in the midst of personal crises, people for whom a 24-hour hotline is a part of their mental health plan and those who just need to talk. These experiences serve as an avenue to use my talents and abilities to investigate with an impact and a purpose. Each aspect of one's life is influenced by others and in turn has its own impact. Researchers such as Dr. Nicholas are asking: Why? How? What if? The program is going a step further and asking: How can this be applied? Is it effective? As part of the University of Wyoming program, I can contribute to the investigation of these questions while developing skills to put theories into practice.

Ana Reid
Lesley University

Dominican Republic native and former stay-at-home mom, Ana left high school early and earned her GED. Shortly afterward, she enrolled in college courses but became discouraged because English was her second language, and she was taking a lot of remedial English courses. "I did not accomplish my goals," she says. "My high school and the college counselors utterly failed me even though I had the burning desire to make it."

Ana enrolled in a non-accredited, three-year theology program and later raised her children at home for 10 years but still had a desire to go back to school to earn her bachelor's degree. She says that there was a difference between applying to college as a young adult and applying as an adult student later in life. "I did not possess the necessary support that a 16-year-old girl needs. I did not have any kind of orientation or a sense of direction. I just knew that I wanted a college education. As the years went by, the more evident it became as to what to pursue in school."

Being a single parent, Ana admits that balancing school and family can be challenging. "I had to accept that I could not do it all," she says. To help make sure her children get additional individual attention, she got involved with the Big Brother and Big Sister Association. Her son has a "big brother" and her daughter has a "big sister" who give them individual attention and get them involved in fun activities. Of course, as a good parent, Ana also makes what she calls "Mama time" to ensure her children spend time with her even with a demanding school and work schedule.

Currently, Ana works as a program director at Citizens for Adequate Housing, a homeless shelter in Peabody, Massachusetts. She eventually wants to earn a master's degree in social work to continue helping others.

Ana's Essay

Since an early age I have dreamed of getting a college education though no one in my family or extended family had done so. The part that was not clear was when, how, where, as well as what course of study to pursue, but time and life experience have shed some light on that matter.

I was born to a family that was very giving and community oriented. My grandparents raised 12 children, eight grandchildren and other children from the community whose parents could not afford to provide for them. I was among the eight grandchildren. Our home, which sat in a small valley surrounded by hills in the Dominican Republic, was the center of the community. Don Coro y Dona Casilda, as everyone addressed my grandparents, donated the land where the chapel was built. The one-room school which provided education up to third grade, the highest grade most of the people in the community acquired, if that, sat on our yard.

Besides raising a big family, my grandparents also provided medical attention to many. No, they had no medical training, but they had learned to survive in that semi-remote part of the country. I remember several elderly people who were regulars. When they were feeling poorly, they would come to be nursed back to health. When someone had no food, Mama and Papa would somehow come up with something to help out.

Hard times came to the family, and a window of opportunity opened for my oldest uncle to come to the United States. By the early eighties the whole family had migrated, but through the years

Mama and Papa's legacy continued. Whenever a member of the family returned for a visit to the farm, he or she would go through a lot of trouble to bring goods to the community.

Migrating into this new industrial and prosperous land brought many blessings but also much pain and many hardships. The family structure that once brought comfort and security was suddenly gone, and nobody was really in charge. The younger ones who still needed parenting and much attention were forced to fend for themselves and learn to survive on their own, as the adults worked long hours in hard labor. I was one of those younger ones, lost in a turbulent sea and with no one to point the way. Life was very difficult and painful; it still hurts to think back.

My schooling, which was so important to me, was disrupted over and over again. I went from school to school and in the process missed out on a good and solid education. I fell through the cracks. How I wished for a good student counselor or a teacher who would take interest in me, but they failed me. I was just one more in the middle of a decaying school of an impoverished and needy Hispanic community. At age 16, out of profound frustration and panic, I left school, took the GED and ventured into college that same year. Due to poor and uninformed choices as well as to uninvited cards that life played me, I did not accomplish my career goals and shame set in.

Since then I have accomplished many things of which I am proud. I completed a three-year diploma program at a theology school, I took random courses here and there, I hiked the Appalachian Trail and I produced two wonderful children, but I never got the education I so much longed for.

Through the years I contacted many colleges and universities and cried in many school offices, but no school would accept the credits from an unaccredited school except those that my school had made a prior agreement with and which were no longer options for me.

In 1998, during the second most turbulent time of my life, the end of my marriage, I did another round of meetings with schools in New England, and after many tears, I came to terms with the fact that there was no way around it. I needed to start almost from square one.

After being a stay-at-home mom, which was an enjoyable and valued experience, I was forced to enter the job market to support my family. For a couple of years I worked at Gordon-Conwell Theological Seminary as a research assistant and registrar assistant. At the seminary I worked among scholars who were concerned about issues regarding life and community. Here my mind was greatly stimulated, and the desire to pursue higher education burned within my heart. My second job was working for the Association for Retarded Citizens as a family resources coordinator. This was my first official job working with families in need. Here I got my feet wet. It was a very rewarding job. I learned to love and respect my families, and they were very affirming. By now I had a clearer picture of the route I wanted to take.

Presently I am the program director for a homeless shelter. It is a very good fit for me. I have the opportunity to make a difference in people's lives in a way that is most rewarding. I am able to work on empowering families and individuals to rebuild their lives and move forward. I have found that the hardships that I have been exposed to or that I have personally endured have prepared me to relate to a lot of the issues and struggles that many of the families that come to us have.

It did not take me long, however, to realize that I needed further training in many key areas to be successful at what I do, but what about the barriers that so firmly stood in the way?

I am a survivor of a 12-year, emotionally abusive marriage. It has been a very long and painful journey. I have emerged but not alone. It took a lot of support, encouragement and confrontations from an army of family, friends and professionals that rallied around me. It took their objective words and their genuine care to give me the strength and the courage to take some very hard steps. Though the road was hard and most undesirable, I would not trade all that I have learned and how I was enriched. I have felt the despair, the feeling of being trapped with no way out or no easy way out. It is my desire to continue to be part of that army who rallies around people in need. I am bilingual as well as bi-cultural, attributes that have greatly helped me in working with my clients. These skills will also be a great asset for my future goals as I carry on the legacy of my grandparents.

The turbulence died and the sea leveled: it was time to pursue my dream. This is where Lesley came in. The program in human services with specialization in management combines my life passion with the necessary skills needed to put it into practice.

So far the "Lesley Experience" has been a wonderful, enriching and hope-imparting one. The shame that had been so entrenched is slowly eroding away and pride is taking its place. I don't think the school has or will ever have a more enthusiastic and grateful student than I am. With its adult program, Lesley has broken down the barriers that blocked me from moving forward. Being part of a cohort enhances the experience as it renders the opportunity to develop lifelong friendships with colleagues who have a heart for the same line of work I possess.

It is my goal to ultimately get a master's in social work. I see myself speaking to groups of people, especially women, and offering training to help empower individuals and to inspire them not to give up but to move forward in life. It is my desire to instill hope in people by pointing them to resources and by sharing my story and the stories of those who have succeeded. There is also in me the remote dream of helping establish an orphanage and a library in my hometown in the Dominican Republic. The role I wish to play is in the area of public relations, public education and fund raising. Lesley offers in my program of choice the tools and skills I need to make my dreams and goals a reality by laying a good and solid foundation, preparing the way for the next steps in my professional and educational journey.

Jacqueline Holmes
University of Akron

When Jacqueline Barnes Holmes first attended college, she was recently divorced and a single parent with two children to raise. She managed to make her education a priority and earned a bachelor's degree from Kent State University in Ohio.

Then for 22 years, Jacqueline worked for the local public electric utility company. She was promoted several times, and her most recent job was as a corporate trainer and effectiveness consultant for the internal business unit of the corporate headquarters.

Upon retirement from the company four years ago, she rekindled her passion for education. She entered a master's degree program in technical education with an emphasis in training at the University of Akron, in Akron, Ohio. Because she wants to work as a consultant, Jacqueline decided to stay in school and pursue a doctorate in secondary education with an emphasis in technical education and is now half way through the program.

Although Jacqueline says that applying for college the first time as an adult student was frightening, she says that it was easier than applying at a traditional age. "Right out of high school, I wasn't focused on much of anything except fun."

Her focus is different now. After finishing her Ph.D., Jacqueline's goal is to work as a consultant trainer for her former employer.

Jacqueline's Essay

Upon completion of my master's degree in technical education, I am requesting admittance into the doctoral program in secondary education with emphasis in technical education. I hope to enter the program in the fall semester. For my dissertation, I plan to extend the research on the differences (if any and to what extent) in actual classroom practices between pedagogy and andragogy.

Two years ago, I left my job to pursue a master's degree in technical education. For the last five years of my employment, I worked as a corporate trainer in the company university. In that capacity, I conducted seminars in diversity, change management, team leadership, team problem solving, conflict resolution and process improvement. In addition, I had limited experience in performance consulting with internal business unit leaders.

Although I was competent in my job and enjoyed my work, I realized that I did not have adequate skills or the formal education necessary to compete successfully on the open market in the area of training and development. I realized I needed to become more competent in conducting needs assessments, designing curriculum, developing knowledge and performance-based assessments and computer technology. I also felt I needed knowledge in the theoretical and philosophical foundation of my discipline.

Upon completing my education, I plan to re-enter the workforce as a training and development consultant. According to the Occupational Outlook Handbook, a Ph.D. is an asset in consulting work. Twenty-two years of experience in human resources in a public electric utility coupled with five years of training experience and a doctoral degree should give me a competitive edge in the consulting marketplace.

Stephanie Kriner
George Mason University

Stephanie Kriner always dreamed of getting a master's of fine arts degree in writing. While working as a journalist for the American Red Cross, she covered the terrorist attack on the World Trade Center on September 11, 2001. That day changed her life. She wanted to have a bigger impact. She wanted to take her writing a step further than her day job. She is now pursuing a master's degree with a concentration in creative nonfiction at George Mason University in Fairfax, Virginia. With her passion for writing, Stephanie wants to "tell stories, especially stories about people who otherwise would have no voice," she says.

As an applicant to a graduate writing program, Stephanie's admission essay had to be even more unique—it had to reflect her voice as a writer in addition to convincing the admission committee to accept her. "Because I was applying to a creative writing program, I wanted to write my essay as a story," she says. "Also, I wanted my words to evoke my passion for writing and my desire to shift from journalism to creative nonfiction."

Writing with passion is something that Stephanie advises all students to do. "Use the essay to sell yourself while at the same time revealing that you are human, that you have a real passion for whatever degree you are pursuing," she explains. But she also cautions students "not to apologize for anything, even if you are worried that some weakness will keep you from getting into the school."

Stephanie's Essay

While covering the terrorist attacks in New York the week of September 11, I felt guilty for being a writer.

One day, I rode along with a group of Red Cross volunteers delivering meals to rescue workers and people stranded without food near the wreckage of the Twin Towers. I snapped the volunteers' pictures as they struggled to carry heavy boxes of food and containers of steaming coffee to a group of elderly people. I interviewed a volunteer, a woman in her late 20s who lost 12 friends in the disaster. They were all firefighters. Her boyfriend was a firefighter too, but he had survived and was still working the rescue effort at Ground Zero.

Despite her losses and anxieties over her boyfriend, the young volunteer displayed an inspiring passion for her work. She forced me to question myself: How was I helping?

I have stuck with my chosen profession since graduating from James Madison University with a bachelor's degree in mass communication in 1995, but doubts such as these often arise. As a reporter for the American Red Cross, writing stories for the websites Redcross.org and Disasterrelief.org, I have been forced to question how I can remain a bystander, an observer surrounded by people bringing assistance to disaster victims.

In New York, I felt especially guilty for running around with nothing more than pen, paper and camera as others delivered relief. I felt ashamed for being afraid that the dust mask I wore was not enough to keep the asbestos out of my lungs, while I was surrounded by volunteers, firefighters, doctors and police officers who labored on without complaint.

Every night, I sat alone in the sudden quiet of my hotel room. I stared out my 21st floor window overlooking Times Square and allowed myself to absorb the horrible things I had seen that day. I would finally let the tears fall for a few moments, and then I would type the day's story into my laptop. I wrote about a group of Manhattan residents who cheered and handed sandwiches to rescue workers, a woman who refused to accept that her brother had probably died in the collapsing World Trade Center and the volunteer who lost her fire-fighting friends.

There were so many stories to tell.

Yet, in the midst of such great need, I could not see how my words would make a difference. When another reporter replaced me in New York, I went home to Washington, D.C., feeling that I had somehow failed.

Back at Red Cross national headquarters, I continued my work, writing about the Pentagon relief efforts and the pending refugee crisis in Afghanistan. I was inspired by the outpouring of support, the large number of hits to the Red Cross websites and the new energy my coworkers had for their jobs. Still, I kept thinking that there must be more I could do.

One day about a month after September 11, a coworker just returning from New York told me about a volunteer who had asked about me. The volunteer turned out to be the one who lost her 12 friends. My coworker said that the young woman wanted to thank me for the story I wrote about her and the other volunteers. She also said that I had been a "big help." I was not sure what she meant, but the words forced me to smile. Somehow, I had created an impression on somebody.

That is when I recalled—as I have many times before—why I had chosen this profession. I love to write because it allows me to connect with other people. Over the past seven years, I have written for a weekly newspaper, a business newsletter for funeral directors and finally for the Red Cross websites.

The message from the New York volunteer made me recall others who have shown their appreciation through the years. I remembered a middle school basketball coach I interviewed in Warrenton, Virginia, who was nervous that I would misquote him. After the profile I wrote about him appeared in *The Fauquier Citizen*, he sent me a thank you note, saying I had made a difference in the community.

I also remembered a woman in Venezuela who was ashamed to tell me about how she became a prostitute after losing everything she had in the mudslides of December 1999. Afterward, she beamed when I assured her that readers would find her ability to overcome the predicament inspiring. She grinned proudly and would not let go of my hand as we said goodbye.

Yes, indeed. I have touched many lives. How could I stop writing now?

In fact, I want to go a step further—to connect with readers in a more intimate way by writing creative nonfiction. I want to share my own experiences. Although my background is journalism, I am confident that I will grow into a talented creative nonfiction writer while a student in George Mason University's master's of fine arts program. The degree will allow me to pursue my goals of writing essays and other stories for publication and teaching other aspiring writers.

It may seem like I am taking a major leap. At the beginning of this essay, I wrote that I felt guilty for not giving more. Now I am expressing a desire to partake in a particularly selfish form of writing: focusing on my own life and reflections. However, I realize that good writing connects people by helping them understand other viewpoints—whether they are my own or somebody else's. As I have just pointed out, I have learned to connect with people through their experiences.

Now, it is time to share my story.

Susan Moloney
University of Buffalo

Many people give up when life poses significant challenges, but not Susan Moloney. At the age of 16, Susan dropped out of high school. She obtained her GED, but she entered a life of addiction to heroin and alcohol for the next 20 years.

When a friend enrolled in a master's of social work program, she explains, "I said to myself, 'I want to do that!'" Susan then started at community college, battling Hepatitis C while she studied for her bachelor's degree in social work at Buffalo State College. She has been in remission from the disease since 2000.

Susan spent much of her time volunteering while obtaining her social work degrees. She volunteered at the Boy's Club, the Cornerstone Manor, a mission for women and Attica Prison, in addition to her social work internship with the county's Child Protective Services department.

In May 2003, Susan achieved her dream. She earned her master's degree in social work from the University of Buffalo and is on her way to making a difference in the lives of disadvantaged and at-risk youth. Susan is a shining example that with perseverance, anything is possible.

Susan's Essay

Social work has appealed to me since I was a teenager. I remember wanting to join the Peace Corps to help underprivileged children disadvantaged by their birthright. Drawn into the wild life of the early seventies, my dreams disappeared. At 46 years young, I now feel I have an abundance of personal knowledge accompanied by an education that is beneficial to my serviceability to others.

My main field of interest lies with at-risk kids and juvenile delinquents. The criminal system is also interesting to me. My life experience lends to the ability in understanding what these particular youths rebel against and the life problems they face.

Five years ago I discovered I had a serious illness, Hepatitis C. One year later I began treatments for my illness along with my first year of college. I was off and on treatment until June 2000, when I went into remission. The treatment was very debilitating and at times, I wanted to give up on school. Somehow, I made it through. I attended North Country Community College in Lake Placid, New York, in 1996. In that first year, I won the Laurie Fons award given to an outstanding student showing promise in a social work career. At the end of my second year before receiving my associate's degree, I won an award for most college spirited. I had been active in our outdoor activities with our school float for the winter carnival held each year. This was quite an accomplishment for me, winning awards, considering I had never graduated from high school. (I did however earn my GED in my early twenties.) After graduation I became very ill due to the treatments and decided to return to Buffalo to be near my family. I then applied to Buffalo State College as a social work major. It was not an easy time. My grades have not been exemplary due to my illness. With perseverance and faith, I have made progress.

In August 2000, I began my internship at the Erie County Department of Social Services at Child Protection Services. My tasks involved helping clients to find adequate housing, filling out rental applications and working as an advocate to get other needs met, such as security deposits, furniture and public assistance. In working with one of my clients, we encountered many obstacles; it was one thing after another. If the client did not find adequate housing soon her children would not be returned to her. I was discouraged at times and felt as though the client was unmotivated and unwilling to do her part. My supervisor noted that the client may have certain barriers blocking her cooperation. It was revealed that the client owed so much money to utility companies she could not receive any services. I called an abundance of agencies for assistance such as Salvation Army, Neighborhood Coalition and Catholic Charities. Once we got the utility problem resolved, the client was intimidated when speaking to a prospective landlord. I suggested a role-play and it helped the client immensely in obtaining an apartment on her own. I learned a lot about myself working with this client. For instance, I should not be quick to make a determination when I do not have all the facts. I have learned to explore the whole person and to look for barriers that may stand in the way of success.

With all due respect, I have had a difficult time putting this together. I can write an "A" paper with ease, but this, as important as it is, was very hard. I know I am a great communicator, an active listener and a truly empathetic person. I also know I am becoming a good social worker. I am a divorced single parent, with an 11-year-old child and have dealt with a debilitating illness and survived. These experiences have only added to my strengths as a social worker. In the next five years, I would like to work in a program with adolescents or early teens.

Jennifer Barr
Bryn Mawr College

Jennifer Barr was accepted to Boston University (BU) straight from high school, but she decided to defer her admission and worked at a bookstore in her hometown. After a year of working, she decided not to attend BU and continued working for another year before enrolling at the University of Michigan. "While it was an excellent school, it was not the right fit for me—it was much too big," says Jennifer. She took classes for about two years and didn't feel committed to school so she dropped out and began working in the technical writing and editing field. Ten years later, Jennifer returned to her dream of going back to school after being laid off—proving that sometimes things really do happen for a reason.

Jennifer heard about the McBride Scholars program at Bryn Mawr College, located on the outskirts of Philadelphia, from a friend. At Bryn

Mawr, she is pursuing a bachelor's of arts and is focusing on East Asian studies, an interest that began when she studied Chinese at the University of Michigan. Her previous education did not go to waste—she was able to transfer two full years of academic study from the University of Michigan that will count toward her Bryn Mawr degree.

She hopes to continue to graduate school and would like to work in Chinese linguistics studies, teaching the language or translation.

Jennifer's Essay

Walking into a bookstore or library has never failed to pack a special punch for me. I see the shelves and shelves of books and know that each one could lead me to a landscape I've never seen. A room filled with books covers such a wide range of human endeavor and interest; it has always amazed me.

During this application process, looking through the course catalog has felt a lot like looking at a wall filled with books. As far as the eye can see, there are titles to pique the interest.

I have always read a lot. Reading and absorbing information are things I do well. However, I would like to improve my analytical skills and critical thinking. Pursuing a degree will hone my ability to use information to define and solve problems and make me a stronger defender of my opinions. I can't think of a better place to do these things than a college that offers a wide range of liberal arts courses.

Studying in an environment where each student and professor holds a unique viewpoint and a unique collection of knowledge is very appealing. A liberal arts program offers a set of tools that are broadly applicable. In my career, I have worked with people who hold degrees in highly specific technical fields and with people who have had a broader general education. In my experience, the "generalists" are more flexible in the work they can (and will) undertake and are better at adapting to change. They're also usually more lively lunch companions.

Another factor that draws me to a liberal arts college is that my parents both attended one. It's rather obvious to say that my parents have had a big influence on me. But in fact, they are both very intelligent people who are always interesting to talk to. Another thing that's true of both of my parents is that their careers have been deeply and enduringly satisfying to them. My mother is a recently retired elementary school teacher, and my father is a pediatrician who studies birth defects. Both of these lines of work are difficult, challenging and continuously changing. They're also both important to the well-being of a society. I consider each of these factors something to aspire to in my own work and my studies.

I am applying to Bryn Mawr for several reasons. It is a highly respected and rigorous school that will provide me with a thorough and solid education. It is a small school, and given my past experience as a member of the huge student population of the University of Michigan, I see that as a distinct benefit. I've read about and attended a presentation on the McBride Scholars program. Everything I've learned makes me believe this program will provide the support and structure I need to get the most out of my education. Finally, Bryn Mawr is emotionally appealing to me. My mother graduated from the college, and I'm excited about the prospect of continuing a (long-suspended) tradition.

Erin Darling
University of California-Santa Barbara

Erin Darling has had an interest in the environment ever since she can remember. She attended Colby College in rural Waterville, Maine, immediately after high school and studied environmental policy. While she was there, she had the opportunity to spend a semester in Ecuador conducting environmental research. A couple years after graduating, Erin realized she needed a more focused education on current environmental issues to obtain the types of jobs she wants. "I have found that the best way I can make a difference is to educate myself so I can teach others and share my knowledge," she says.

Now, Erin is studying for a master's degree in environmental science and management at the University of California-Santa Barbara. In Erin's experience, like a lot of others, the process of applying to graduate school is significantly different than applying to college.

"It took a lot more initiative for me to apply to graduate school than it did to apply to college," she explains. "College was something I always knew I would do. Graduate school was my choice alone, and I had a lot less guidance in the application process." She had been working as a naturalist, teaching skiing and traveling and was in a different mindset than she was right out of high school.

She is interested in studying water issues and the effects on people, flora, fauna and species conservation and would eventually like to open an environmental studies center and run conservation efforts and environmental education programs as well as outreach efforts in the community, tying in her interest in organic agriculture.

Erin's Essay

My interest in the environment began at an early age. When I was in sixth grade I spent a week at an environmental overnight camp where we studied the equation: E-C-D-C-I-C-A. The formula stands for the following: Energy, Climate, Decomposition, Change, Interdependence, Conservation and Adaptation. Each day we studied a different part of the equation. I can recount almost every moment of that week I spent in the wilderness. As I have grown older and have had the opportunity to study in more depth the ideas that were presented to me at the camp, I have become a strong advocate of conservation, sustainability and environmental education.

I went on to study environmental policy in college. The first class I took on campus was a sustainable development course where I researched environmental issues in Honduras. Other classes that made up my major were an environment and society class where I studied the Great Lakes Drainage Basin, an environmental law class and environmental economics. In my senior seminar I researched the environmental and safety conditions of the Maquiladoras (foreign-owned factories) that lie on the border of Mexico and the U.S. It was a paper that required original research and interviews with employees of the U.S. companies that produce goods in the factories. My studies at Colby inspired me to travel abroad in order to gain more field experience.

I spent the spring of my junior year participating in a comparative ecology program in Ecuador. I studied in the rainforest, the cloud forest, the high country, the coast and the Galapagos Islands. These ecosystems make Ecuador, a country the size of the state of Colorado, one of the most diverse in the world in plant and animal species. Unfortunately, the country is threatened by constant environmental destruction. I spent a month living with a family in a rural village where the common practice not long ago was to burn the land in search of carbon and use chemicals to grow food. With the help of an organization called Maquipacuna in Quito the town has become a successful example of a localized environmental movement that has not only brought life to the land but to the people as well. I researched the impact of this organization on the town, helped maintain an organic garden and funded and managed the construction of a greenhouse.

In my travels in the United States I have seen the same urgent need to clean up the land and fight to prevent environmental destruction. I recently read an article in which a leader of the environmental movement and former U.S. Forest Service employee stated that "it is not oil and gasoline that are the diminishing resources, it is [open space and wild places]." I grew up just south of San Francisco and have been astounded by the changes and growth I have seen with each visit home to the Bay Area in recent years. I now live in the Roaring Fork Valley in Colorado, a place where land is also diminishing rapidly. It is my desire to research sustainability and the possibility for economically viable conservation in order to save what open space we have left.

When I graduated from college I was hired as a summer naturalist intern at the Aspen Center for Environmental Studies. I led nature tours, helped run the 25-acre nature preserve and developed curriculum for environmental education classes at the center. Aspen is a small town surrounded by four wilderness areas, yet the threats still exist. Through my work with ACES I have helped people see beyond the tourist attractions of Aspen to the true beauty of the valley.

I have much to offer the Bren School of Environmental Science and Management. I am dedicated to my field and eager to devote myself to research and studies in sustainability and conservation over the next two years. I work very well in a team-centered environment but am also driven on my own to succeed in projects and research. My field experiences as well as my undergraduate academic studies have led to my decision to pursue a master's degree. I am excited to get back to school and begin study and research in my chosen field.

Adelle Rochester McDermott
Wellesley College

Adelle Rochester McDermott had a successful career in the travel industry for more than 20 years but always regretted not going to college. So when her chance presented itself, she "seized the opportunity." Adelle is now studying for a bachelor's degree in liberal arts at Wellesley College, a women's college in Massachusetts as an Elisabeth Kaiser Davis Scholar.

Adelle chose Wellesley because she wanted a well-rounded education since she plans to pursue a law degree and work in public policy one day. "I had only experienced working in one industry my entire life, and when I contemplated changing industries it became quite clear that I did not have the educational credentials to do so," she explains. She quit her job in Texas and moved back to her home state of Massachusetts to attend Cape Cod Community College before transferring to Wellesley.

Adelle feels that writing the college admission essay is extremely important in the college admission process, especially for adult students.

"Writing an essay reflects not only your ability to communicate in written form but also how you view yourself," she explains. "To write an honest autobiographical essay takes deep introspection and reflection. Not only will the essay show that you are capable of overcoming obstacles, the writing of a good essay is an obstacle unto itself."

In the process of writing her essay, it turned out differently than she intended. "I revealed much more of my distant past than I thought that I would," she says.

Adelle feels that the admission process "can be overwhelming and frustrating," but nevertheless, has this advice to give to future students: "At times you will think it's never ending. Stay calm, be organized, and don't panic. Many people have done this before you and have survived to talk about it."

Adelle's Essay

My story is most likely the same as many women who were raised in the same time period that I was. Post-secondary educational opportunities were not as prevalent as they are, thankfully, today. What makes my story unique are the choices that I have made and the results realized from those choices.

I'd like to think that I have the intelligence and skill not only to leap the hurdles that come my way but also to learn and grow from them. My early family life laid the foundation for survival skills but did not necessarily support academic pursuits. I did well academically and athletically through junior high school. But by the time I reached high school, my home life started to deteriorate and so did my interest in academics. I am certain that my high school transcripts reflect this.

Unfortunately, my father passed away a month after I graduated from high school. My family's financial situation was not good, and any thought of college had to be put aside. While I worked full-time in a clerical position, I dreamed of becoming a flight attendant. I saved up enough money to attend an airline training school in Connecticut. The education that I received was focused on the entire travel industry. My flying dream vanished quickly, and I chose another career path.

My travel career began in recreational travel. Eventually, I decided to change to corporate travel. In anticipation of this I enrolled in the Certified Travel Counselor Work/Study Program for Travel and Tourism sponsored by Institute of Certified Travel Agents. The courses covered sales, personnel, business principles and marketing. I earned my certified travel consultant designation and began working with travel agencies that managed travel programs for large corporations.

Over the years my career advanced eventually leading to an executive management position. This necessitated a move to Dallas and represented a very big step up in my career. I like to refer to that time of my life as my "accelerated educational period." Every day brought something new. The pace was high-speed, and the challenges were enormous. I learned about politics, cultural diversity, diplomacy and performance beyond any of my expectations.

Up to this point in my life, my biggest regret was not attending college. While I was successful in my personal life and business endeavors, the lack of a formal education was always in the recesses of my mind. After much introspection and with the support of family and friends, I took a step that altered my life. I moved back to Massachusetts and enrolled at Cape Cod Community College. Since then, I have been inducted into Phi Theta Kappa and placed on the dean's list. I will be earning an associate's degree this spring. It has been a wonderful experience and has given me renewed confidence to attain more academic accomplishments.

What an achievement it would be if I am selected for admission and continue my undergraduate academic experience at Wellesley College.

Nancy Davies
Vermont College

Nancy Davies went back to college at age 45. The experience made her realize that a lot of other adult students could use a supportive environment. She was so passionate about the need for adults to have a place to find information that she launched AdultStudentCenter.com four years ago, a year after finishing her B.A.

Nancy always wanted a degree, but like many other students, life circumstances put it on hold. "I always intended to get a degree," she says. "It was a promise I made to myself to go back."

In addition to her website for adult learners, Nancy is pursuing a master's degree in organizational psychology with a focus in adult learning. Now in her mid-fifties, Nancy hopes to one day use her advanced degree to work with companies as a consultant on topics like adult education, strategies for success and incorporating life-long learning into daily living.

When it comes to writing the essay, Nancy says, "It's not what's right or wrong or good or bad, but it's how well you express why you want to go back to school, what you will do with it and what your interests are. They really want to see who you are."

Nancy's Essay

I am an avid gardener. Over the years, I have lived in several houses, giving me the opportunity to create more than one garden. The first were just for me—private retreats, tucked away in a corner of the yard. Now my very public garden completely surrounds my house, reaching out to passers-by. Its beauty is more in the pleasure it gives others than in the solace it gives me.

My education mirrors my evolution as a gardener. I went back to school to develop myself and my career. Faced with increasing use of technology in my marketing job, I returned to college at the age of 46 to study information systems, together with business and psychology courses. After five years of part-time study and full-time work, I received my bachelor's degree, summa cum laude. While I was able to put my new skills to work immediately on my job, I gained much more than skills. I discovered an unexpected interest, adult education and a desire to work with, and on behalf of others, to facilitate their personal growth through education.

A year after graduation, I pursued my new interest as a hobby with the launch of a website, www.AdultStudentCenter.com. My goal is to provide a community for adult students, a place they can share experiences and get information. When I started, I had just 15 newsletter subscribers. Now more than 650 students, prospective students and adult educators have signed up to receive the Learning Circle, my email newsletter, and many more visit the site. My hobby has turned into a passion. I hope to encourage even a few adults to go back to or to stay in college.

Now I want to return to college to develop myself even further but also to better enable me to share my efforts with others. My professional goal is entrepreneurial as opposed to corporate or academic. I would like to form a group to work as a liaison between business, school and community to expand support systems and educational opportunities for adults beyond the traditional classroom.

Although I am very pleased with the feedback I get through the Adult Student Center, I know this is only a small step toward fulfillment of this goal. Last year, I had the chance to work part-time at my alma mater Marist College as an adult student recruitment and retention counselor. It was a wonderful opportunity to put my marketing skills and my passion for adult education to work with adult students. Unfortunately, the job was cut short by the 9/11 events. In the economic aftermath of this tragedy, I had to devote more time to keeping my primary employer's start-up companies afloat, and I just couldn't keep up the pressure of two jobs. But I did gain extremely valuable experience in the five months I spent at Marist, working with adult students face-to-face.

I feel that my personal experience as an adult student, the experiences of others shared with me through the Center and Marist College, and my extensive research into resources available for adult students have given me a good understanding of the issues involved in adult education. But I know that I don't have an adequate grasp of the theories that will provide a solid foundation for creative solutions to the problems I've encountered. That's why I want to study for my master's degree with a focus in adult learning and development. I also want to continue my studies in psychology to give me a better understanding of group dynamics, interpersonal and group communications, self-efficacy, autonomy and motivation.

The most pressing issue I have encountered and the one I want to grapple with in my studies is how to better integrate continuing education with adult life, especially work life. This is the area—this small, but growing, overlapping space between corporate education and academia—that I believe holds the most opportunity for adult learning. I think my studies in adult education and psychology will best prepare me for involvement in this space. However, I feel they should be augmented by an understanding of organizational development issues. Over my 25-plus years in marketing, I have been involved in facilitating internal and external communications with many companies. Some of this work, especially communications audits, touched on the areas of knowledge management, training and human resource development. But I seek deeper knowledge of business cultures, especially from the perspective of the individual's development and contribution.

I was introduced to Vermont College by an alumna who has generously volunteered her time to help me in the Adult Student Center. I am excited by what I have seen of the college, and I'm looking forward to experiencing the Vermont College model of adult education. It perfectly suits my need for a flexible curriculum. I have searched extensively but have found few other appropriate programs. Many adult education programs are geared toward teaching, basic education and literacy;

organizational development programs offer too little depth in human development, and I'm not interested at this time in achieving certification as either a teacher or psychology practitioner.

I have no qualms about my ability to succeed in independent study. My orientation is toward work, whether for my living or for personal fulfillment. Although work fills up a large percentage of my waking hours, I find that so many of my ideas and projects relate to each other, it's not hard to balance work, study and hobbies.

Throughout my career, I have worked most effectively without much supervision. As a freelancer, I have conducted market research, developed market profiles, prepared marketing plans and marketing communications programs. As a project manager, I have located and managed internal and external resources and developed and monitored budgets and schedules. Since I do much of my work from my home office, I am able to make my own hours. This is another reason, however, that I need a flexible, self-directed learning program.

If accepted into the master's program, I should have no trouble finding resources with which to pursue my studies. Although I work primarily from home, my office is located in New York City so I have access to all that the city can offer, including libraries, associations and conferences. Of course, I also have the web. Typically, I start my information searches on the web to find industry associations, key players, people and books that lead me to more extensive resources. I am a member of the American Association of University Women (AAUW) and the Association for Non-Traditional Students in Higher Education (ANTSHE).

I'm ready to go back to school. I've spent the past two years urging others to continue their education. Now it's time for me to listen to myself. I have come to education late but with dedication. I hope you'll allow me to pursue my dream through Vermont College.

Deena Lewis
Lesley University

Deena Lewis is a former stay-at-home mom who is now going back to college to become a guidance counselor. Her first time going to college was at the age of 22, when she started an associate's degree program.

On the one hand, Deena wishes she had gone to college right after high school. On the other hand, she sees the positive aspect of pursuing higher education later in life—she now knows what she wants to do. She says, "I look at what I have been through and feel I had to experience what I did. I had no idea at 18 what I wanted to do with my life."

Deena chose to attend Lesley University in Boston because of its weekend program. Also, her former credits were transferred to her degree program, and she has received credit for life experience. She recently wrote a paper worth 10 credits based on her prior life experience.

Because of her demanding schedule of caring for her three children and going to school, Deena needs flexibility in her work as well. Last year, she worked as a substitute teacher. "That was good because it is a per diem job," she says. It also gave her experience in education—and that may also help her when she applies for the guidance counselor job one day.

Deena's Essay

I am in the process of beginning a new life for myself, which includes my three children, ages 3, 6 and 15. Over the last several months I have had to consider what road I'd like my life to take and how my children and I can most benefit from my choices. For the past five years I have been a stay-at-home mom, after giving up an advancing career in the corporate world in downtown Boston. My two young daughters quickly became my priority, as well as being a housewife after I stopped working. Being at home enabled me to give my daughters the care and attention they needed, and I have prided myself at being able to be at home with them. I have been involved with their activities, trips to the library, school field trips and play dates and volunteer my time at their schools. I take a very active role in their lives and often describe that involvement as being their lifeline to this world. I can honestly say I am proud to have such a role.

Unfortunately, my husband and I separated last year and we are going through a divorce. This past year has been incredibly painful for me but also an awakening. My marital separation came on the heels of my grandmother and father's deaths within nine months of each other. Needless to say, the past two years have been an emotional roller coaster for me, but I was able to maintain motherhood to the best of my ability. Throughout my separation, I have been able to continue to stay at home, but the reality of my situation has left me with the conclusion that I need to start thinking about me and what I want to do with my life, while still giving my children the stability and consistency they need.

The reality that I need to further my education is clear to me. It is something I planned to do some day anyway, as my children got older. The only decision I had not made was what will I go back to school for and my major. While considering my children first, I came to the conclusion that I would like to have a career where I am working with children. My thinking has always gravitated toward this idea; I just didn't know in what capacity I might want to accomplish this. I decided that a job or career that would allow me to be available to my daughters when they are not in school would be in their best interest. I considered becoming a teacher but felt my calling was in another area. I only recently thought about becoming a guidance counselor, and I have grown very comfortable and excited by this potential career path.

The next hurdle I came across in my thought process was how I am going to attend school, do homework, study and still be an effective mother. This was very overwhelming to me, and I seriously wondered how I'd be able to accomplish such a goal. It was ironic that I recently received a mailing from Lesley that offered open house dates. I couldn't help believe this was a sign, and I should take advantage of the opportunity to learn more about Lesley. By attending the open house, I discovered the wonderful off-campus program; I knew this was something I couldn't pass up and could work into my life with little disruption. I feel I have some direction on where I can go with my education and career while still mothering my children. This is truly a gift to me to have such a wonderful opportunity. I have been excited by the idea of going back to school, especially at Lesley.

I love telling people my plans to go back to school and hearing their reactions. So many people don't understand that it is possible to expand your mind and your goals while continuing to be an attentive mother. The off-campus program Lesley offers is like no other program I have ever heard of. Lesley can help fulfill a dream for me, and I am grateful to have such a challenge before me. When I graduated from Northern Essex in 1994, it was an adjustment for me not to have to go to school. I missed attending classes and interacting with the students and professors. It was a place where people were eager to learn and get something more out of their lives. I am looking forward to being in those surroundings again and am eager to be a positive example to my daughters. I want them to see what a woman can do with her life on her own. I hope they grow up seeing my inner strength, determination and accomplishments. This may help them to see their own potential as young women and encourage them to strive for more in their lives.

I will end this personal statement with a tender moment I recently experienced with my six-year-old daughter. After giving her a bath and helping her get ready for bed, she said to me, out of the blue, "Mommy, can I be you for Halloween?" I was shocked and uncertain as to why she would ask such a question but smiled at her and asked her why. Her reply was, "Because I love you." Her simple statement touched me deeply and also helped me to see that when I am passionate about something I do it well.

Nicole Jennings
Smith College

Nicole Jennings, a former figure skater, caught the acting bug right after high school. But after finding out what the acting world was really like, going on audition after audition and memorizing lines, she decided it wasn't for her. "I thought to myself, I can't do this for the rest of my life," she says.

Because Nicole's role model is Gloria Steinem, a Smith alumna, she always wanted to attend the college. When she found Smith College's Ada Comstock Scholar program for non-traditional women students, Nicole knew it was for her. "I was offered a scholarship and couldn't turn down such an opportunity," she says.

Nicole is currently studying for a B.A. in psychology with a focus on the psychology of women and gender. She eventually wants to work in some capacity connecting women with the media. Recently, Nicole has done an internship with Oxygen Media, the women's television network. She is considering several career options like working for a women's magazine or starting her own women's non-profit media foundation to create educational films about how media affects women's lives. "I want to help women feel good about themselves," she says.

Nicole's Essay

It is 5 a.m. as I roll out of bed. It's still dark outside and I am half awake as I get dressed. My mom yells, "Hurry Nick. The taxi's downstairs." I grab my books and carefully run down the hard marble stairs of our brownstone and hop into the car. Upon entering the rink the smell of the morning mist permeates my lungs. I go to the locker room to change my clothes. The cold air makes me stiff as I put on my tights, dress, sweater, gloves and skates. I grab my scribe and head to the ice ready to do work. After concentrating on figure eights intensely for 45 minutes, freestyle practice begins. I warm up my body by doing laps around the rink—forward crossovers and strokes then back crossovers and strokes, increasing my speed as I skate. Now I am stretched, warmed up and ready to practice. I work on my spins, jumps and footwork before attempting my 2½-minute choreographed program. By the end of the session I am gasping for the moist ice rink air. Both tired and exhilarated, I change my clothes for school. At 7:45 a.m. I get breakfast at the diner on the corner, and then I am off to school. At 3 p.m. I head back to the rink for my 4 to 6:45 p.m. session with my coach. Both on and off the ice we work on my stamina, technique and program. Afterward, I go home, have dinner, do homework and go to sleep. This was my daily life for eight years—and I loved it.

Now as a college student, I feel that I can fully appreciate all that skating has brought to my life. There are many parallels between my life as a skater and that of a scholar that have given me the confidence needed to face the everyday challenges of higher education. My endeavors at school have called for me to be disciplined, ambitious and patient. However, I have discovered that life is a little more complicated. Skating helped me in many ways but in one particular way it did not.

When I was in high school I missed days and sometimes weeks of classes during competition time. During those periods I trained on the ice six to eight hours a day. Missing so many classes made it really difficult for me to catch up with the other students. In addition, during my freshman year in high school, I lost two very important people in my life. A friend of my mother's who had always been like a father to me died of AIDS. Then a year later I lost the only grandfather I had to a heart attack. This was a devastating time for my mother and me. I tried to be strong and continue. My mother became depressed and in many ways I lost her too. Although this period in my life was a lot more complicated than I can express in an essay; it negatively impacted my learning.

After having to give up skating because of forces beyond my control, I took an interest in acting because I missed the performance aspect of skating. The two-year Meisner program I completed trained me for the many rigors of the acting business. After doing numerous small roles and walk-ons, I achieved what I thought I wanted when I got the lead in an independent feature film. However, after receiving the script and starting rehearsal I realized that I didn't like what I was doing. Even in independent films, women are frequently judged by what they look like and not who they are. Overall the process left me feeling empty. I subsequently turned the role down and decided to give up acting.

After assessing my life and realizing I had limited job skills, I decided to realize my dream of going to college. Not only was this a difficult decision considering what I had been through, but at this point in my life I was living on my own, working as a waitress and paying my own bills, with no savings, no SAT scores and bad grades in high school. Who was going to accept me? How was I going to pay for it?

Then everything turned around for me. I knew that if I wanted to go to college that I had to take things step by step and just as in skating, I needed to be focused, patient and diligent. I took on extra shifts at work and started saving the money I needed for tuition. Most of my summer was spent meeting with tutors I had hired to help me brush up on writing and learn some of the algebra I missed in high school. I took the CUNY entrance exam on which I attained a perfect score on the math portion. This news made me feel wonderful. I was accepted into the Borough of Manhattan Community College.

During my second semester I discovered something interesting about myself. I gave a persuasive speech on why people should be less tolerant of street sexual harassment. When I stood in front of the class and began to speak, I became filled with passion. I spoke about the problem of street harassment and how it affected my friends and me. After the speech, I thought a lot about my genuine interest in the issues of women in today's society and realized that I could be an effective advocate. In another class I wrote a research paper on Kate Chopin and her use of liberation in three different short stories. It was in this research that I asked questions and analyzed early contributions to the women's movement. The combination of these assignments and my personal life experiences led me to my current interest in women's studies. Although I have a lot to learn on this subject, I start from a place that is sincere, eager and passionate.

The Borough of Manhattan Community College has offered an excellent beginning in my education. It has also given me the opportunity to find intellectual enthusiasm. My efforts at BMCC are both recognized and appreciated by many of my professors. I consistently go above and beyond my assignments. Consequently, I feel I am ready for the educational challenges that a college such as Smith offers. As I present myself as a candidate for the Ada Comstock Scholars Program, I bring with me years of hard work and experience as a result of my dedication in many areas: skating, education, employment, internships and volunteer work. From the moment I walked onto the Smith College campus I felt at home. I know that attending Smith will provide me with the supportive educational atmosphere I need to realize my professional and personal aspirations. I hope to make an important difference in whatever I do in life, and I think Smith College can provide me with the skills I need in order to accomplish my goals.

Traci Warner
William Mitchell College of Law

Personal experience led Traci Warner's path to law school at the William Mitchell College of Law in St. Paul, Minnesota. While serving as a paralegal and going to school at Evergreen State College in Washington state, her son's father filed suit against her when the state of Oregon attempted to garnish his wages for child support for their son. With paralegal skills under her belt and help from an attorney at the firm she worked for, Traci tackled the suit head on and it was dismissed in the preliminary of stages of the case. She won.

"I found my forte in the law," she says. Eventually, Traci would like to "hang up her own tile" and combine her interests in family law, intellectual property law (human genome specialty) and do legislative work. But most of all, Traci says she wants to be an advocate for other individuals like herself.

Traci's Essay

I sat before my computer, as I did so many times before, meandering through the different governmental web pages to get to the case file online. I did not have any prior knowledge of how long a Federal District Court Judge took to make a decision on pre-trial motions, but 60 days seemed excessive to me. Because of the delay of the decision, I thought maybe my file was lost or that the Judge was in the process of denying my motions and it was time to hire an attorney to defend myself in trial.

I am a single mother who has spent the past 11 years raising my son without the help of his father. When the prosecuting attorney's office in Oregon found my son's father and proceeded to establish child support and garnish his wages, he filed suit in the Federal District Court in Eugene, Oregon, against me. His claim was that I inflicted emotional distress on him by denying him his parental rights. He asserted because of the emotional stress he suffered he was entitled to $350,000. The case was spurious and potentially damaging to my family.

I was working as a paralegal in a law office in Tacoma, Washington, after receiving my associate's degree in a legal assistant program, and I had just started my junior year at Evergreen State College. I was quite busy. Many nights I would stay awake searching the Internet and many Sundays I would spend at the law library researching Oregon and Federal law. The attorney I was working for agreed to come into the case if it got too tough or went to the next stage after pre-trial motions.

I also elicited the help of another attorney who worked for our firm as a legal researcher and writer. I brought him my research and we sat together and planned our strategy. We decided that we would prepare and file three pre-trial motions. In the back of my mind I thought about my own experiences as a paralegal and how I had learned that the law was not always fair to people who do not have sizeable resources, so I was leery of what might be the result in my case.

If I lost a lawsuit in Federal District Court and a judgment was filed against me, I would have to wait years to be able to afford law school. I wanted to study the law, and I know my passion for justice would help to give my children and me the foundation we needed for the future. If I were able to graduate from law school, I would acquire the power that knowledge and socio-economic freedom brings. And in return, my goal will be to help others like myself or to help those who need a voice within the judicial system.

I found the website with the listings of court filings in my case. On the top of the page, it stated that my case had been dismissed. My heart leaped. I scrolled down to the last entries where I read, "Motion to dismiss for improper venue, denied; motion for a more definite statement, held as moot and motion to dismiss for failure to state a claim, granted." I had won. Having the lawsuit dismissed in the preliminary stages not only confirmed that I had done the right thing by protecting my child, but winning also substantiated that I was on the right track in my life. If I had not acquired legal training, knowledge and contacts, I wouldn't have prevailed in defending myself.

My mother has always asked me what I was going to do for society. I have always tried to help those in need, but throughout my life I knew I was meant to do more. I am now fully aware of what I am going to do for society and where my journey will lead. I am going to continue to work hard and to acquire additional legal training, knowledge and contacts so that I may speak for those who cannot.

Laurel Stachowicz
Smith College

Dance has always been Laurel Stachowicz's first love. She first attended college at the University of Massachusetts for three years before she became pregnant with her first child. At UMass, she was active in taking dance classes and teaching and continued to do so even after she left the university. One of her accomplishments outside of the academic world was becoming a successful choreographer in Boston.

In spite of her accomplishments, Laurel decided to go back to school because she needed the personal fulfillment of getting her degree.

"When I was younger, I did not have the self-confidence to pursue a dance degree, but since I decided I was going to make the huge decision to return to school, I figured I should do what I love and take full advantage of my opportunity," she explains.

Laurel is now in the Ada Comstock Scholar program for adult women at Smith College and is pursuing a B.F.A. in dance performance and choreography. After Smith, Laurel plans to continue practicing her passion—dance. Only this time, with a degree in hand, even more exciting opportunities in dance should come her way.

Laurel's Essay

"Mommy, you're going back to school!" she exclaimed with the kind of excitement and wonder as only a four year old can. I was surprised at how much pride filled me at her response. It has always been my intention to return to school and finish my degree, but as a mother of two little girls, plans for myself have been put on hold. Now that my youngest is starting school I decided it might be a good time to realize my goal. Her response convinced me.

I have been a mom since the age of 22. I was in college at the time. Having my daughter Molly and then another daughter Nyssa changed my priorities. Being at home with my daughters became most important. My focus needed to be raising my children with a sense of self-confidence in a loving, supportive environment. My own education, however, has never been far from my mind. I continued to take one or two classes at a time when I could. It proved to be difficult. I took one class while I was pregnant. I went into the hospital to have my baby causing me to miss the final two classes of the semester. Despite the fact that the faculty was aware that I was pregnant and I expected to deliver during the semester, I received an F because of those two absences. I also had difficulty arranging classes when daycare was available. Night courses were limited. I grew discouraged and began to lose my motivation. I wondered if it would ever be possible for me to complete my degree.

At the same time, I built a choreography career. I opened my own dance studio, the Laurel Conrad School of Dance. I learned to organize all the various requirements of producing a show. Besides teaching and choreographing dozens of dances for more than 100 students, I costumed all of them, acted as set and lighting designer and managed all business aspects.

I also began choreographing for theater groups. I started out working in small community theaters. I discovered that I loved creating musical theater choreography and worked my way to professional companies. These companies taught me how true theater works. They taught me discipline and how to work within the parameters set by the Actors' Equity Union. I recognized how much I want to develop and refine my skills and knowledge in choreography. A 30-year-old mother, however, has a difficult time being taken seriously as a dance major. The fear of hearing the words, "You are too old" kept me from applying.

In 1998, the Railroad Street Youth Project contacted me. This was a new program started in Great Barrington for at-risk youth. The concept is to give the young adults of the town a constructive way to use their time. Their first project was the play *Suburbia*. Though this show required no choreography, the company needed someone reliable and experienced in theater to stage manage for them. For the love of theater, I accepted. After taking on the project and getting to know the people involved, I found that I could use my skills to help better my community. After each performance, the director and cast held a post-show discussion. This provided a forum for a dialogue between the community and the youth. The blue-haired, body-pierced, punk kid spoke and was heard. I was encouraged when he said that he didn't have time to do drugs because he was a part of this program. Working on this project tremendously raised the self-esteem of all involved. I contributed. Inspired, I went to area high schools and volunteered to work with the students on their shows. I made sure they learned more than just dance. They learned teamwork, learned respect for themselves and each other and gained self-confidence. I realized that I wanted to use my talents to make a difference in my world as well as be successful in my career.

I gained experience running a business, choreographing and working with youth. As a result I became more self-confident, more focused on my goals, more passionate about those goals and re-motivated to finish my degree. I want to excel in my choreography career. I am eager to master new skills and knowledge. I want to make a difference in my community so my children's world can be a better place in which to live as little girls and as grown women. I want them to see that education is exciting and that hard work pays off. I am ready. I want this for me, not because it is what society expects of me, not because a guidance counselor or parent says it is what I should do but because it is what I want. And I want to achieve these goals at Smith College.

The excitement that my four year old expressed when I told her I was trying to go back to school was the same excitement I felt when I learned about the Ada Comstock Scholars Program. The more I learned about the program, the more enthusiastic I became. Each visit to the campus has been nothing less than warm and welcoming. I was overwhelmed to find that Smith College not only accepts mothers like me but also proactively embraces us. Ada Comstock Scholars have a sense of belonging not only within the program but also within the entire student body. They are made to feel that the school values them. Becoming an Ada Comstock Scholar and finally earning my degree from Smith would develop my choreography career, teach me how to be more effective in changing my world and show my children and me that I can do it. Am I nervous? Absolutely. I would be stepping out of my comfort zone. That would make the accomplishment all the more rewarding.

Vidula Plante
Lesley University

Vidula, who was born in Calcutta, India, comes from a family of teachers. Although her parents were fluent in English, Vidula learned Bengali as her first language. Her family moved to North America when she was four, and she was educated in the U.S. and Canada until she returned to Calcutta for bachelor's and master's degrees in English in her homeland. When she decided she wanted to become a teacher, she went back to school a third time for a B.Ed. from Brock University in St. Catharines, Ontario, Canada. Her decision to become a teacher stems from the fact that it is a family tradition and from a life-changing personal experience. When Vidula was in India studying for her first degrees, she and some classmates were so moved by the plight of child workers that they founded a literacy project.

Vidula is currently a seventh grade English teacher in Massachusetts but is back in school for a fourth time. "After teaching for four years, I wanted to learn more about how to help struggling readers so I applied at Lesley University for a M.Ed. in curriculum and instruction with a specialization in literacy," she says.

Vidula's graduate program is structured to meet the needs of working adult students. She attends classes at off-campus locations on the weekend. She chose Lesley University for its flexibility.

Vidula exemplifies life-long learning. When she finishes her degree, she may go back to school once again—for a degree in reading.

Vidula's Essay

I love to learn. This love of learning has enabled me to make some unusual life choices. Indeed, it was such a choice that led me to teaching as my profession. And it is my desire to excel in my chosen profession that shapes my goals and has, ultimately, led to my seeking admission at Lesley University.

I can trace my desire to be a teacher to the time I spent in India after graduating from high school in Ontario, Canada. I traveled to Calcutta, West Bengal, because having grown up in Ontario, I wanted to learn more about my Indian roots. I knew that my fluency in Bengali, the vernacular of West Bengal, would assist me in adapting to the culture. Once there, I found that the best way to immerse myself in the culture was to enroll in college. I would end up staying to complete my B.A. and M.A.

How does my decision to study at an Indian university connect with my decision to become a teacher? The connection lies in what I did when class was not in session. While a student in India, some classmates and I initiated a literacy project for child workers in the tea stalls and snack bars around the campus. Disturbed by the plight of these children, we organized everything from location to financing.

An important part of this project became arranging the curriculum. Most of the children, between the ages of 6 and 14, worked every day of the week except Sundays. Thus, we had to meet the challenge of making our Sunday afternoon school an attractive alternative to other leisure activities. Mindful of our students' needs, we did not confine ourselves to textbooks alone but opted for an integrated approach that included games and other outdoor activities. It became my responsibility to purchase and distribute teaching materials and to assist in the development of the teaching program. Thus began my initial interest in teaching, which was further nourished by another volunteer experience in India.

Through contacts I made while participating in the grassroots literacy program, I became involved with Sachetana, a women's organization which literally means "Awareness." Sachetana provided concrete assistance to underprivileged women in an effort to make them self-sufficient and thus less open to exploitation. This was primarily achieved through training in marketable trade skills. Recognizing, however, that an effective awareness program cannot run on training alone, Sachetana also offered other facilities such as medical and educational assistance. My duty there was to provide the girls with an exposure to other cultures. Using myself as a case in point, I was able to introduce them to the concept of multiculturalism, especially as it is practiced here in North America. This group of about 14 girls, between the ages of 10 and 20 (and most employed as part-time domestic helpers) were eager to learn about foreign countries and unfamiliar, snowy climates. Using this interest as a base, I was also able to address deeper issues such as those of race and gender. It was at Sachetana that I discovered my aptitude for working with large groups of students. Again, this led me to consider teaching as a profession.

My work with underprivileged children in the literacy project at Jadavpur University and with older girls at Sachetana generated challenging situations where I had to be receptive to the conditions of my students. The primary focus was to maintain a high degree of motivation among the students, thus ensuring their attention (and attendance). When I left India, I brought with me a strong desire to continue my work in this field.

Back in Canada, I applied at and was accepted into the teacher preparation program at Brock University. The one-year program provided me with the basic framework necessary to be a successful teacher. Upon graduation, I began my professional career at an inner-city school in Ontario. Although equipped with my middle school English teaching degree, I was not equipped to deal with the number of students I came across who lacked basic literacy skills.

One particular student stands out. He had been enrolled in our middle school in January of his sixth grade year and so had been attending for half a year when he entered my seventh grade English class. I was extremely surprised to see that "James" could not read or write. I referred him for testing, but while waiting for his turn on the extensive list, it became clear to me that James needed to be provided with work that would challenge him at his level. Otherwise, his self-esteem suffered, leading to progressively disruptive classroom behavior.

Being educated as a middle school teacher, my knowledge of how to foster rudimentary reading and writing skills was limited. I spent much of my after-school time gathering information that would help me to work with James. Although James was an extreme example, I came across sufficient numbers of students having difficulty with reading and writing to make me consider getting some formal training in this area as well. This feeling increased when I moved to Massachusetts.

For the last two years, I have been living and teaching in Massachusetts. For both years, I have administered the seventh grade English MCAS assessments. Here, also, I faced situations where I felt that an increased grounding in literacy basics would have been of great assistance to me. It was during this time that I began to look for a master's program that could provide me with such a focus.

I shared my desire for professional development with my principal during a goal-setting meeting, and he suggested that I consider Lesley University. In looking at the course offerings, I was impressed with Lesley's flexibility and also with the master's degrees it offered in the field of education. I was drawn in particular to the curriculum and instruction, because it covered the two major professional development areas in which I was interested: literacy and curriculum.

Although the preceding paragraphs explain my interest in the literacy portion of Lesley's program, they do not explain my interest in curriculum. Having been educated at a teacher's college in Ontario, I am fully versed in the language arts program requirements for that province. When I began working in Massachusetts, I made it a point to acquaint myself fully with the Massachusetts Frameworks. Being one of two seventh grade English teachers in my district (and the only one in my school), I was encouraged by administration to take my knowledge of the frameworks and use it to develop a seventh grade English district curriculum. Although this was a task close to my heart, I felt that some further training in curriculum and instruction would assist me immensely in doing the job well. Thus, I was pleased to find that Lesley offered a program, which seemed so suited to my needs.

In these paragraphs, I have outlined my enthusiasm for learning and traced how that enthusiasm was channeled towards a desire for learning in specific areas. Through my experiences, I have learned that the basic principle of teaching is a teacher must be a learner first. I feel that my receptivity and flexibility, along with education and training at Lesley University, will professionally equip me to address the needs of my students. I thank you for considering my application.

Jennifer Warren Glacel
Virginia Commonwealth University

On paper, Jennifer Warren Glacel has it all: a program manager job with AOL Time Warner, her own condominium and a supportive family. But in the past year, Jennifer noticed something was missing. Her career simply wasn't fulfilling, and she wanted to do more. After some serious soul-searching, Jennifer decided that her future would be in a helping profession. "I was inspired to go to graduate school because of a need to do something more with my life," she says.

As a girl, she volunteered as a Girl Scout, which she found immensely rewarding, and she continued volunteering in college. So she decided to apply to master's of social work degree programs even though her bachelor's degree from William and Mary is in an unrelated field.

Jennifer is now attending Virginia Commonwealth University's graduate program part-time while working and looks forward to becoming a social worker. Her story reminds all of us that sometimes, experiences from childhood hold the keys to the future.

Jennifer's Essay

Who am I? I am 27 years old, a homeowner and car owner; I have a well-paying job, a great boyfriend, a wonderful family and good friends. But something is missing. Despite my past enjoyment of my job, I have recently become frustrated and dissatisfied. This frustration led me to look at how I have arrived at this point and where I should go from here. I have never had to consider this before—to look at my life and evaluate and come to any conclusions about where I should be going.

My life has always been full of change, although I have rarely been the catalyst for the change. As an Army brat, I spent much of my life moving around, changing schools and settling into a new town, a new life. My dad would get a new job and off we would go. One of the constants in my life as my family moved around was the Girl Scouts. In each new town I would join a troop of girls who would work together to make crafts, go camping, earn badges and help others. I was a Brownie in Alaska, a Junior and a Cadette in Virginia and a Senior in both Virginia and California. I earned the Silver Award, Gold Award and the Silver Trefoil, a special volunteer award only given in Virginia.

I decided when I was three that I wanted to go to William and Mary, so choosing a college was not really a decision. In college, I joined a sorority in my freshman year and immediately became very involved, especially with my sorority's annual fundraiser, a week of activities to raise money for the National Association for the Prevention of Child Abuse. During my junior year, I was in charge of the entire week, leading approximately 100 people working in committees to host each event. We raised around $3,000 for this worthy cause.

Following my graduation from William and Mary, I went to work for Congressman Ike Skelton. I had interned in his office twice before and was offered the job even before applying for it. As I did not know exactly what I wanted to do, this seemed a good way to start exploring. I began as a staff assistant and was soon promoted to be the Congressman's scheduler. During this time, I lived with three of my closest friends and got used to life on my own in a city. What I did not realize at the time was that one of the things missing in my new life was volunteer work. I understand that now as I look back. It had been a constant with Girl Scouts and then in college with the sorority. So I organized my friends to participate in DC Cares and the National Race for the Cure.

During college, my mother was diagnosed with breast cancer. My family was living in Belgium at the time, and I was home for winter break when she got the news. I did not want to return to school in January, but my parents were adamant. I felt powerless to do anything to help. So when I graduated, I got involved with the National Race for the Cure. I volunteered in the office as well as participated in the race itself with friends and family every year. One year, my roommates and I organized a happy hour at a bar in DC. We raised over $1,000 for the race by asking patrons for donations. When my parents moved to the DC area, I convinced my Mom to participate in the Avon Three-Day Breast Cancer Walk. She and I walked 60 miles and raised close to $12,000 dollars. Over the next two years, my family and I raised over $25,000 for the cause.

After nearly two years working on Capitol Hill, I knew that it was not where I wanted to be. I enjoyed working for Congressman Skelton, and I was good at organizing his days and trips, but I was no longer learning or growing. I actually planned to continue working for him for another year, but an opportunity presented itself at AOL. Leaving the Hill and going to AOL was more about timing than a real decision.

I arrived at AOL with little specific computer knowledge but with a desire to do something new and to learn. I have spent nearly three years working my way from an administrative assistant to the head of the team that does the technical work allowing the AOL software to be released by marketing. I have enjoyed the learning and growing to this point, but I am now realizing that I do not feel fulfilled by my work here and I am growing increasingly frustrated because of that. Now that I am comfortable in my position and I no longer have new things to learn, I am again noticing that something is missing.

Throughout my life, family members and close friends have asked if I ever have thought about being a psychologist, therapist or something in the helping field. My first answer was that I had not given it a lot of thought. Then, I realized that if I truly thought about a new direction in life and I found it that I would have to act on it. I have always been the type of person to act on something once I decided on it. To think about a change that I felt was the right thing meant to me that there would be no turning back, and that would mean turning my world upside down—going back to school, changing jobs, making a big change of my own making.

As I realized all this, I knew that it was finally time to think about what I should be doing. So I thought about the area of psychology, social work and therapy. Then I thought about my current and past work. I believe that what is missing right now is helping others. As I look at my past activities and work, the skills of organization and leadership have always been my strong points. Looking closer and thinking about the things I have enjoyed most, I realize that I get the most enjoyment and fulfillment when the work that I do helps someone else. My frustration levels rise and I become dissatisfied when I feel I am no longer making a difference or a contribution.

Working for a large company that is increasingly concerned about the bottom line and less and less concerned about employees has underscored this feeling of dissatisfaction. I am not helping anyone, improving lives or making a difference. I recognize that helping others is very important to me and that the corporate life is not where I want to stay.

Realizing this, I began looking at graduate programs in the area. Without a background in psychology or social work, I knew I would have to go back to school. My mom had always encouraged me to go back to school for a higher degree, but I always said that I did not want to do that until I had a purpose for going. And now I feel I have a purpose.

A part-time MSW program seems to be the right answer for me. It would allow me to turn my life upside down slowly, not all at once. In researching what was required for an application, my vague feelings of the MSW being the right thing for me began to solidify, as I have read and now understand the NASW Code of Ethics and the core values of social work. They correspond to the way I live my life, and I realize that they are missing in my current work. What I want in my life, for my career, is something where I can impact other people's lives, even in just a small way.

I remember one day when we lived in California. It was the first day of spring and gorgeous outside, and I was in a wonderful mood. As I drove home I passed a homeless man on the street, begging for money. When I arrived at home, I packed a bag lunch and drove it back to him. The small things that we can do for each other as humans are what make the big things worthwhile. As I remember this moment, I realize I would like more of them, and the difficult ones that come with them.

Heather Neal
Smith College

Heather Neal didn't need a college degree to succeed professionally in Manhattan. Born in Ireland, she started working with her father during high school and learned everything about the printing industry hands-on. She quickly proved herself and rose through the ranks. Among Heather's reasons for making a life change was the stagnation in her industry, her ennui at work and the constantly on-the-go Manhattan lifestyle.

Her interest in massage parlayed into psychology. During several client sessions, she ended up listening to her clients' emotional problems too—and she discovered she enjoyed listening to people work through their problems. She now wonders, "Why didn't I do it sooner?"

Heather's ultimate goal after Smith is to become a psychologist. More specifically, she would like to connect her interests in massage and psychology. "My interest lies in the relationship between touch and the mind. Perhaps developmental or health psychology would allow me to counsel and touch people," she says.

Heather's Essay

To me, life is one big classroom, and until recently, where I did most of my learning. I was born and raised in Ireland before the school reform, during a time when women's roles were limited. The wealthy had many choices, and the poor had few.

Both my parents are artists. Dad used to be a banker until he was told, shortly after WWII, that he didn't have long to live due to head trauma from a bomb blast. He decided to follow his dream of being only an artist, and the family followed along. Ten years after my father was supposed to die, I was born into an eclectic family. My parents created a design business from our home, and whatever the project at hand, the whole family took part. This is where my early learning began.

My insatiable curiosity continued throughout my childhood. Because my sisters and brother were older, I spent a lot of time alone, wandering along the cliffs, beach-combing and working with the locals. I learned how to fix fishing nets, set moorings, patrol the village, birth calves and tar boats by tagging along with the respective professionals. In my parents' business, I learned how to make signs, build floats for St. Patrick's Day and make architectural models.

At about six or seven, my home became an all-female household when Dad left for America to design some Irish pub interiors in New York. At the time, Ireland was in a depression and money was tight. Dad worked three jobs in New York City in order to send money home to us. Once he got his green card, he applied for ours.

In 1979, we moved to New York. We sold everything we owned and started a new life in Spanish Harlem. Dad had a huge apartment in a building full of Holocaust survivors. He was the superintendent of the building. I helped do chores around the building when I wasn't in school. The tenants became fond of me and often invited me in for tea and a chat. I learned so many things, from correctly reciting Shakespeare in a theatre to understanding the courage, strength and faith of a Holocaust survivor. A year later, we moved to Long Island where we bought a house that we completely renovated while Dad started his own sign business and I finished high school.

In school, I was popular but aloof. I had one friend and lots of acquaintances. I was part of the student government, a member of the speech and debate team, vice president of the yearbook committee and involved in counseling other students about smoking and drinking. However, when graduation came along, I was unprepared for the next step. At the same time, I worked as a shift manager at a gas station and worked helping my Dad when I wasn't in school. I didn't know what I wanted to do with my life, and we certainly didn't have the money to pay for me to figure that out in school. We all contributed money to the household from our respective jobs.

During the course of working together, Dad and I became friends. He was amazingly open and smart and always learning. Logic was his best skill. He taught me to look at a project and figure out ways to make it more efficient. His unique perspective allowed me to grow and develop independently. He applied for me to be a layout artist at a local Pennysaver News. When I was interviewed, I told them that I had done this before in various forms in my Dad's business—so they hired me. I quickly became engrossed in the advertising, design and printing business and rose through the ranks until I outgrew the company. I took the next leap and got a job at a trade magazine closer to the city. Eventually, I moved into my own apartment. I worked my way through two more jobs until I found myself at Pluzynski/Associates with a reputation as an excellent layout artist. I was just turning 21.

When I started, there were only nine people working there. When I left, 12 years later, there were 90. I started as a freelance layout artist and left as director of technologies. As the industry changed, I adapted and thought proactively about the next few steps the company would take. My managers saw something in me and knew that I had great potential. They gave me the freedom to try new things. They fostered my growth in the business market and my curiosity about the technologies market. I presented my ideas and pursued them, and I succeeded most of the time. My manager became known for being on the bleeding edge of technology, and I was responsible for it. We worked as a close-knit team. I was involved not only in the production of the catalogues but with estimating, budgeting, projections and new business pitches. I educated clients like Cartier, Alfred Dunhill and American Express about their production processes. In the business, my name had a good reputation behind it.

I tried to attend school while at Pluzynski, but the demand on my time at work was too much so I had to forego taking classes in order to make a living. The few classes I managed to take at Hunter College made me thirsty for more education, but I was caught in the vicious cycle of meeting deadlines and staying ahead of competitors. Twelve years later, the company was running like a well-oiled machine, and I was getting bored. Changes in the industry were calling for smaller budgets, and in response, like many companies, we started downsizing. I volunteered to be laid off in order to seek other challenges. I knew if I didn't leave I would be stuck there forever, highly paid but mentally bored and with little time for anything but work.

I went back to freelancing and found that I was still bored. During this time, I stressed about paying bills and living in the city. Meanwhile, I had a new friend who had been diagnosed with terminal cancer.

Thomas was 28, married and had a two-year-old son. Over the course of a year, I traveled down south to see him, and in that process, I learned to see the world again. He celebrated each day, noticed the sky and the air and enjoyed life to the end. Even though he and his family were broke due to the expensive cancer treatments, they were happy. Thomas' last words were, "I have everything." I asked myself what I had, and I didn't like the answer. I decided to change my life. I listed all the things that made me happy and came up with a plan to move to Northampton within a year in order to become a massage therapist.

I worked hard in my last year in New York City. I freelanced at American Express Creative Media as the production manager and took on the short-term challenge of re-constructing the department more efficiently. I did such a great job that they offered me over $100,000 to stay. It was hard to refuse the "golden handcuff," as my supervisor called it, but I knew I wouldn't be happy. Six months later, I was enrolled in massage school and had relocated to Massachusetts.

I adjusted to school very quickly. I was working four nights a week in a restaurant in Framingham, living in Lincoln with my sister and traveling 90 minutes to and from school each day. The workload was intense, but I loved every minute of it. I graduated with my massage certificate and a 3.95 GPA. I loved school so much that I decided to stay at G.C.C. to get my associate's in healing arts. In massage, I soon noticed that many of my clients spoke of their personal lives and problems while being massaged. I also noticed that I had a large number of clients who were on medication for depression yet still suffering with it on a daily basis. I took psychology in order to understand a little about the workings of the mind. I was hooked. I decided to continue my education in order to become a psychologist. During this process, a friend mentioned the Ada Comstock program, and today, I am writing an autobiographical essay for my application.

How is my academic background different? Well, my learning has been very un-academic in the sense that much of it took place outside of an institution. I worked to support my family and myself, and I still help support my parents today. As a child, I apprenticed in order to learn. My dad created constant change in our family, and I responded by adapting and integrating my experiences and learning in order to advance. I learned cultural integration at an early age, when we moved from a small fishing village to Spanish Harlem. As an adult, I created stability and dependability yet constantly sought challenge and knowledge in my life and my career. I surrounded myself with people who could push me mentally, those from whom I could explore new ways of thinking and learning. Despite all my non-academic learning, the excitement I have sitting in a classroom, learning something new is irreplaceable—I value this education more than anything. At 33, I wasn't afraid to change my life completely in order to seek education. All my life choices and their outcomes have facilitated my growth and learning up to this point. When I graduate, I will be the first person in my family to have obtained a degree—better yet, to have a degree from Smith College! Once I realized that not only could I go back to school but that I could do well, the possibilities for my education became endless. Why stop at a B.S.? I am planning on getting my Ph.D. in psychology and combining mind and body work in an effort to decrease human suffering.

I feel that I am prepared for the rigors of a Smith education as I have spent the last three years in school, working two, sometimes three jobs and I am a straight-A student. Since I started school I have been on the Dean's list every semester. I live locally on a very tight budget and have prepared for this next step as best as possible. When I graduate, I intend to use my B.S. to get a job teaching massage and ethics for massage in order to finance further studies in graduate school. I look forward to being a Smith Ada Comstock student this fall and am excited at the prospect of more education in my future.

Tara Spence
Wellesley College

Tara Spence, a native of Brooklyn, New York, dropped out of high school in the ninth grade. At first she bounced from job to job but finally secured a position as a bus girl in a local restaurant and eventually became the manager.

Success in the restaurant business gave Tara the confidence to go back to school. She reached the point where she just had to go back because her instincts were telling her to. "I had always felt this void, an emptiness that stemmed from not having an education," she says. "No matter what I accomplished I never felt worthy. I knew I would never feel good about myself until I had earned a degree."

Tara is now in her second year at Wellesley College pursuing a double major in classical civilizations and geology. This is about as far from her original education plans as she could get. When she first went to community college, her goal was to obtain an associate's degree in hotel and restaurant management.

Now Tara's new goal is to attend law school to pursue a career in international environmental law. "I have always been an environmentalist at heart, and now I hope to actually acquire skills to accompany my passions," she says. After she finishes law school she wants to become a voice for environmental concerns. She has had a summer internship with a geologist studying ancient volcanism on the East Coast and plans to research at a lab in Volcano National Park in Hawaii.

Tara says that education is the best gift that you can give yourself. To other adult students, she says, "Have confidence in your innate talents and find the courage to pursue your dreams. You are the only one that can make it happen."

Tara's Essay

I was born to a dysfunctional family who meant well. I was raised in Bensonhurst, Brooklyn, a blue-collar neighborhood where many women with immigrant parents find themselves torn between two worlds. One is deeply rooted in old world customs that cast women in the traditional roles of marriage and motherhood. The other world speaks to women about breaking these bonds. I was raised to be a "good-girl," and good girls don't break anything (especially bonds). Eventually, I realized I couldn't continue to inhabit both worlds; I had to decide which future would be my own. I had three options: I could settle down and marry a nice boy; I could go to that place where most neighborhood girls never go: college or I could find my own way. I chose to spend my life free from the trappings of convention and tried to find my own way. Now I am back to plan B.

My parents divorced when I was three and my mother re-married soon after. Home life was tumultuous at best and a nightmare at worst. My mischief caused great pain to my new stepfather, and I spent most of my time with my grandparents. My grammar school career was golden. Teachers said I was imaginative and showed great promise. Every year we took citywide aptitude tests. In the fourth grade I was the star of my class with a twelfth grade reading level. From the time I could hold a book, reading has been a great escape for me. It is a habit I have carried with me into adulthood. My grandmother, who lived on the Long Island Sound, nurtured the burgeoning intellectual she saw in me. Time spent with her was idyllic for an inner-city child. I often found myself pretending I was an author, and I would write stories about great battles waged against pirates on the shores of the Sound outside her house. I became enthralled with nature and the beauty of the world around me, a great contrast to the concrete starkness of Brooklyn. When I was 12, she died and I was sent home to my parents. I was angry, bitter and in great pain. Watching the only mother

I ever knew die of uterine cancer was a devastating experience. In the years that followed her death, I became a rebellious teenager bent on my own self-destruction. School lost all meaning for me; I became a chronic truant and I was usually in trouble. I was a student at three high schools in four years and never received a diploma.

There I was, a high-school dropout who hadn't even managed to find a "nice boy" to settle down with. I fled Brooklyn and returned to Long Island, the only true home I ever had. I found a job as a bus-girl in a local restaurant and easily escalated to management. That gave me the courage to try my hand in different fields. Repeated successes in the work force restored a lot of the self-esteem that had dissipated during my high school debacle and subsequent hunt for independence, but despite my achievements, I still felt unfulfilled. I decided the only way to put my errant past behind me was to conquer my own limitations starting with the embarrassment of having an eighth-grade education. And so, I began the process of becoming the woman I believed I could one day be.

Becoming a college student at the age of 30 was not something that I had planned. I was established at my job as a restaurant manager and had made career advances that provided some of the security for which I had been searching. In the back of my mind, college was always some unattainable goal like winning the lottery or singing at Carnegie Hall, something that might happen but was probably very unlikely. I thought attending college would be an insurmountable challenge. It was a challenge, one that has shown me everything is surmountable if you work hard enough. When I was a teenager, I seemed to have no attention span. I would sit in a classroom and try to pay attention, but my mind would wander and I couldn't focus. The detailed images of my fantasy worlds seemed more real to me than the facts I was expected to recall on tests. After a while, I just gave up.

I forged ahead with my life, deliberately shunning anything remotely academic. Working in the restaurant business, I came in contact with many college students home for summer break. I felt out of place working with them knowing that in September they would go, and I would remain. My defenses were a saucy attitude and a chip on my shoulder. I thought it was much easier to have Mom and Dad pay for college, as those students did, than to do what I was doing: earning my own way.

Eventually, I realized my cockiness stemmed from jealousy, and my chip was suffocating me. It began as a voice somewhere in my mind that said, "Just do it, Tara. Just go to school." That voice became my mantra, and my mantra became a crescendo, and before I knew it, I was a full-time college student. My first semester was terrifying. I was terrified someone would look at me and say, "You don't belong here. Go back to Brooklyn. Go back to your restaurant, but don't stay here." But every morning I got in my car and drove to school. I learned the MLA format. I mastered linear equations. I knew how to test the validity of databases, and I think I finally understand the struggle in the Middle East. These intellectual endeavors changed my life. I had become a different person in that one semester. I felt accomplished, empowered and smart. When my finals were over I thought I did well enough, but I wasn't sure what my grades would be, and then I realized that it didn't matter. Much to my surprise, I received five A's for five classes and had a 4.0 GPA after being out of school for 15 years. I was on the Dean's List and asked to become a member of Phi Theta Kappa. I now value education above all else and am determined to go as far as I can.

In September 2001, I received a letter from the director of the honors program at Nassau Community College. The letter spoke of Wellesley College and its Elizabeth Kaiser Davis degree program, a "program for women over the age of 24 who wish to work toward their bachelor's of arts degree." My first reaction was pure elation. My second reaction was dismay. It was wonderful that the director thought I was worthy to attend Wellesley, but I was sure I was not. I thought an admission advisor would look at me and laugh, "Oh? Do you think you can turn your back on college for 15 years and then have a shot at attending Wellesley?" I didn't think so, and I was sure Wellesley didn't either.

I went online and began to do research about Wellesley. The "Portrait of a Davis Scholar" seemed to describe me in every way possible. It was as if it had been written as an invitation to Tara Spence. The person who wrote that passage might have seen inside my soul. The last line says, "In the beginning, she probably believes she is the single mistake the admission committee made. She is not. She belongs here." After further research, an orientation and an interview, I also know I belong at Wellesley.

The destruction of our environment has been a cause close to my heart since I was a child. Living in a coastal area, I watch beach erosion daily. The garbage that washes up on our shores has created a wasteland of refuse for beach goers. In our rush to inhabit America's coasts, we have destroyed them. America is defined as a maritime country with 95,000 miles of shores, bays and estuaries that we depend upon. Our coasts are fragile, and rampant coastal development is still a big problem. I don't know what the solutions to these problems are, but I know the answers are essential to the future of our families, our countries and our world.

My views may be idealistic, but I have an urgent desire to reverse this decline. I also know that I need more knowledge and a greater focus to be effective. I believe that Wellesley's Environmental Studies Program will provide me with the knowledge and experience to understand the complexity of our planet and the problems that plague it. I know I am not now a scientist, but I also know I have a voice that should be heard. I think Wellesley's program will both educate and show me how to effect change. I believe in environmental justice, and I believe that a Wellesley education will enable me to make a difference. When I leave Wellesley, I hope to attend law school. I strongly believe Wellesley will help me to maximize my potential, reach beyond my limitations and provide me with the knowledge to make a difference.

Describing Yourself

Huan Hsu
University of Utah

Huan applied simultaneously to the law school at the University of Utah and to the MFA program at George Mason University. Accepted and offered scholarships by both, he is now a student at George Mason.

Huan's Essay

"What are you?" A fellow third-grader once asked me as he pulled back the corners of his eyes with his fingers. "Chinese? Japanese? Americanese?"

"I'm American, stupid," I wanted to say. "Just like you." But was I? Did all Americans have to answer such questions, or wish they looked just a little more like everyone else? Growing up in Utah with the unique double whammy of being not only Asian, but also non-Mormon, I was introduced to self-consciousness at an early age.

My childhood was comfortable, by and large, but I faced reminders of my individuality at every turn—my parents jabbering in Mandarin while shopping, categorical mispronunciations of my name, the only

Hsu in classes full of Smiths and Youngs and Hansens, confusing visits from missionaries despite going to church every Sunday (not the right one, according to them). In my ethnicity I found nothing to appreciate, nothing to glorify, only embarrassment. The fact that my parents, a college professor with the Dallas Cowboys on his brain and a second grade teacher who still makes the best lasagna in town, were far better assimilated than their peers was little consolation. So, in addition to wondering if it was okay to look forward to going to the library or spend entire afternoons with my Legos, I also wondered if it was okay to be Chinese.

Thankfully, my parents also had the foresight to get me involved in competitive sports (though I still had to put up with four long years of violin lessons). Excellence in athletics provided not only a welcome respite from my crises, but also an identity that would serve me for years to come. I made many good friends, learned to apply the concepts we practiced on the field to the world outside the lines, and in the safety afforded by my new identity, the worrying about what others thought of me melted away, replaced by the ability to truly appreciate, understand and accept different perspectives.

The arc of my experience has been diverse, traveling from the homogenous confines of Utah to Tidewater, Virginia, and the College of William & Mary, then up to New Hampshire for summer camp, out to the high-tech business world of San Francisco and now Boston, where I work for the not-for-profit United States Tennis Association and coach Division III tennis. One of the constants has been that ability to slip into another's shoes, and it is what I point to as the reason behind the success I've achieved in each of my endeavors. Wholeheartedly putting myself in another's position allowed me to evaluate how best to affect that person. What would be the most exciting evening program for a cabin full of fifth graders? What angle of a client's story would pique an editor's interest? Which strategies would work best in developing elite tennis players, resolving conflicts and addressing the concerns of parents, players and coaches? By constantly pondering what it was like to be me, I learned skills in understanding what it's like to be someone else.

Perhaps this ability to view the world through other eyes is native to children of immigrants, to compensate for all those squirmy moments of wondering if and where we belong, and for this, I'm thankful. I believe it is one of my abilities that will be invaluable at law school, where I expect many, if not all, of the preconceptions I have about the world will be questioned, where even my decision to pursue a law degree will puzzle me at times. Indeed, taking different approaches, appreciating multiple perspectives, and letting go of judgment helps me study difficult material and cope with stress. And socially, I find that my interactions are much more satisfying when I demonstrate an honest interest in understanding others. Sometimes I wish I was just a little less understanding and could simply dismiss the guy who just cut me off on the Mass Pike as an idiot.

This is also one of the many things that I hope to contribute to the law school community. With more "ABCs" (American-born Chinese) in this country than ever before, I believe my experience is a relevant one. Though the severe culture shock and outright racism that our parents faced are things of the past, my generation deals each day with situations that are no less challenging, searching for an ever-changing identity as we navigate the narrow seam between two worlds, trying to reconcile their sometimes contradictory demands. It's something we practice all our lives, and I feel an obligation to try and show others not only what it's like but how to do it.

What am I? I still wonder, and perhaps the nature of our beings is too dynamic to capture in a timeless, elegant snapshot, as each new experience adds a piece to the gestalt of our identities, and to a larger extent, our country. But I believe the parts of me that I can nail down—my work ethic, my curiosity and desire to exercise my brain, my ability to appreciate different perspectives and communicate ideas—will not only help me survive but excel at the University of Utah. The study of law is not where my search for knowledge ends, rather, where it begins, and I seek an environment where an academically rigorous training in law serves as the common denominator for gaining a greater understanding of the individual lives that make up our collective American experience.

Intellectual Experience

Jennifer Barr
Bryn Mawr College

"Do you want the long version or the short version?" That was the question Glenn would always ask before he launched into an explanation.

For years, Glenn had worked as a welder for an oil company out west. By the age of about 45, he had developed a severe hearing loss and decided to change careers. He moved back to Michigan, where his parents lived, and enrolled in a technical training program. He received his associate's degree in computer science and got a job as the "computer guy" at the bookstore franchising company for which I worked.

My duties at the company were varied. I was an administrative assistant and supported the accounting department. Then I started to help with some basic network and database support for the staff in the office and for the owners of each of the stores. At the beginning, I knew next to nothing about computers.

Glenn, it turned out, was an absolutely wonderful teacher. He was always open to answering questions and was generally happy to interrupt what he was doing to explain fundamental concepts or to help solve a sticky problem.

When it came to learning about the basics of bits and bytes, I usually opted for the "long version." Glenn would obligingly halt the explanation when I'd reached my saturation point, and he would pick up the thread again once I'd processed what he had told me. When I needed to solve a particular problem with a program, rather than give me the answer, Glenn would ask questions—like Socrates or a psychoanalyst—to push me in the right direction: "What do you gain from normalizing the tables in your database?" "What data do you want this inquiry to retrieve?" I got used to reasoning out the solutions I needed. If I couldn't find a solution and got to the point of grinding my teeth and muttering, he would relent and give me a concrete tip to get me back on track.

Glenn was not the first good teacher I've had. I have been fortunate enough to have had many inspiring and effective teachers, in both academic and nonacademic settings. Working with Glenn, however, seemed to flip a switch in me; I became conscious of how I was learning. Previously, I had never carefully considered exactly how interaction with a teacher resulted in increased knowledge or skills.

I began to think a lot about various methods of learning and which were the most effective for me. It was clear that Glenn's approach worked well for me. I was learning a lot and gaining practical skills quickly. His dual approach of explaining concepts and pushing me to figure out solutions became recognizable to me as a technique. The same could probably be said for most teaching styles, but Glenn's style seems to have been particularly parental; he was always there with a reservoir of information, but he encouraged me to tackle the projects I was interested in and to go as far as I could on my own. This encouragement led to an increase in my confidence that I could take on any project and eventually learn enough to do it really well.

Working with Glenn helped me establish an active approach to learning that I believe has stood me in good stead. I am more aware of how I learn, and I have incorporated this knowledge into my work and my studies. I am more confident seeking out information from other people, and I value the satisfaction that comes from working out the solution to a complex problem.

Overcoming Challenges

Juanjuan Blout
Wellesley College

The gloomy moonlight beamed through the rusty bars of the tiny window and lit my run-down brick shack, where the middle school assigned me to live. It was one of many quiet yet agitating nights I spent alone in the early summer eight years ago. I was 21, unable to see the road in front of me that seemed to be so dim and hazy.

Tossing and turning on my bed, I asked myself—tomorrow would I have the guts to tell the headmaster to "teach the students yourself" and walk out of the gate without looking back?

As soon as I came to this middle school in a remote farm town three years ago as a new English teacher, I realized that it was not my dream of life. I couldn't hit the students on their heads with the chalk or twist their ears to force them to earn higher grades in the national exams and hence a bonus for me, as every other teacher in the school did.

I dreamed, every minute, every second, to go to southern China, where people didn't have to live with a secret folder that contained your personal history and that dictated your future, where nobody can be manipulated like a chess piece on the board, where everybody can try new and different things, things they liked.

But dare I, a girl from a peasants' family, think of getting out of a government's arrangement system and dropping out of this big machine? Give up the salary and house I would be guaranteed to my death? Dare I be a defector? Dare I make whole society my enemy and carry the name of a blacklisted person without history for the rest of my life?

I told myself—try to dare to, just for once in my life. And it turned out to be the best decision I ever made in my life. My voice was shaking, and I couldn't even swallow my saliva when I looked into the headmaster's eyes and told him I wanted to be a heretic and I wanted to leave the school. But finally I flew out of the cage like a bird.

Everybody thought I had lost my mind. My father pointed to the threshold of our house and yelled at me never to come back. As the first high school graduate in the village, I was once their source of pride but was now a source of shame.

The most difficult moment was when I was walking away from home on the zigzagging, muddy road, trying hard to hold my tears back and not turn around to my poor mother limping and crying behind me. Carrying a cloth suitcase on my small back, I boarded a Boeing 757 airplane for the first time in my life and arrived in southern China, where I knew nobody and was penniless and jobless.

Six years have passed since that moment, and the days in southern China where I struggled for food and shelter are still as vivid as yesterday. I always feel guilty to have brought such distress to my parents, yet I never regret my decision. I feel proud of myself especially at the moments when I see the smiles on their wrinkled face, when they are sitting in the sun in front of the beautiful house I helped them to build. If I didn't leave the school I wouldn't have traveled up and down the whole country of China and learned so much about life. Moreover, I wouldn't have been able to immigrate to the U.S. and develop my own dreams of life on this free soil instead of living as the timid and negligible puppet of the headmaster's in that remote school.

Life has been good to me, and I think I will continue respecting it and living it seriously and sincerely.

Torah Karuna Bontrager
Columbia University

Torah Karuna Bontrager was raised Amish in Wisconsin until shortly before her sixteenth birthday when she left her home in the middle of the night for good. Because Torah always knew she wanted to go to high school, which is not permitted by the Amish, she decided to live with one of her ex-Amish uncles in Montana. Shortly afterward, Torah began high school and became legally emancipated—the process that allows a minor to be considered an adult before the age of 18.

Torah started her college career at Hesston College in Kansas and San Jacinto College in Texas with a major in aviation to become a professional pilot. "I decided that flying professionally was not what I wanted to do the rest of my life, that I just wanted to fly as a hobby," says Torah. So she left Hesston and began working for an aviation company managing corporate pilots' flights around the world until she was clearer about her future academic focus.

During a visit to Dubai in the United Arab Emirates in 2001, Torah learned about the Humanitad Foundation, a non-profit world peace organization based in London. "I decided that this organization was a perfect avenue for beginning to positively change the future," she says. Torah is now a volunteer art director for the organization. Her work with Humanitad is what inspired Torah to pursue a degree in political science, specifically international political science, with a focus on the Middle East and India at Columbia University.

"I realized that there wasn't much cross-cultural education in the world—at least not in America. For example, the average American doesn't know the history, customs, culture or roots of the Middle East and vice versa, which contributes toward creating misunderstanding, conflict and ill-will," she explains.

After obtaining her bachelor's degree from Columbia, Torah plans to continue her work with Humanitad, create her own organization that specifically promotes cultural education around the world and eventually help Amish kids leave the community.

When she applied to Columbia, Torah used her Amish upbringing as a key part of her essay since she was writing an autobiographical narrative. She says. "I tried to construct my essay around the highlights and turning points of my seven years out of the Amish starting from the beginning and ending with where I was at the time I submitted my essay and why I wanted to study at Columbia."

Here is a letter that Torah wrote to the admission office at Columbia:

Torah's Essay

Dear Sir or Madam,

I was raised Amish with only an eighth grade education given by Amish teachers who, themselves, had never been to school beyond the eighth grade. Because the Amish religion is against higher education and instruction in subjects other than reading, writing and math, I decided at an early age that I was going to leave the life I was raised in so I could go to high school.

Six years ago in May, shortly before I turned 16, I left my family during the night (my parents would never have allowed me to leave if they had known my plans) and traveled by train from Michigan to Montana where I stayed with an ex-Amish uncle, working full-time at a restaurant that summer.

Upon my 16th birthday, I was granted emancipation on the grounds of education deprivation by a Montana district court judge, becoming a ward of the court until I turned 18. Emancipation not only allowed me to go to school, but I was also allowed to sign my own medical releases, enter legal contracts, live independently and obtain a driver's license. The most important thing emancipation afforded me was protection from my parents: they no longer had any rights to me and they could not force me to return to the Amish.

I entered the freshman class in high school that fall, two years after I graduated the eighth grade in Amish school. That year was the first time I ever took a science class, chemistry. Before that, I hadn't even heard of the term H2O. I was a straight-A student that year and at the top percentage of the class. I took the first semester in Montana and the second semester in Wisconsin. I moved to live with my other ex-Amish uncle in Wisconsin so I could work for him in his furniture shop after school hours because there weren't any jobs in Montana during the winter.

During the next term I lived in a different Wisconsin city where I rented my own apartment at age 17. I was planning on taking two years of high school in one, but the principal wouldn't allow me to do that. Instead, he suggested that I complete my HSED (high school equivalency diploma—similar but superior to the GED) that term and go to college the following year. I maintained a full-time job working the night shift in a cheese factory. In the forenoons, I would take the bus to school and work on my HSED classes—I was only required to be in school four hours each day. I was given a lot of independence in how I wanted to utilize my time completing the courses for my diploma so I worked fast enough to finish everything the first semester. However, since I wasn't 18 yet, by state law I had to stay in school. So my guidance counselor suggested that I take a university course, paid for by the high school, to test the waters before I went to college. I took a three-credit English writing class the second semester and immensely enjoyed it. It was then that I felt fully confident that I was capable of fulfilling all of the academic responsibilities a college student had. Before that, I was hesitant to go to college because I didn't think I had had enough of a preparatory education and that the classes would be too difficult.

I went to Hesston College in Kansas during the next term. My chosen major at the time was aviation to become a career pilot. I worked on-campus jobs about 10 to 15 hours a week and rose to the challenge of learning how to fly and at the same time, keeping up with my other classes. I earned my FAA private pilot airplane license in February. That was the first time in my life that I truly felt I had earned something. It was the first time I had to seriously devote time and study and sacrifice to achieve my goal. I got As and Bs in the rest of my classes that year.

I didn't attend college the next fall due to not being able to come up with the extra funding for taking the next portion of aviation training for becoming a commercial or corporate pilot. Instead, I worked and tried to figure out how to continue taking flight classes.

I went back to school in Texas during the spring. I only took aviation classes and started my instrument pilot training. Due to the less-than-desirable flight training structure of the college, I discontinued my flying lessons and finished out the semester with my other classes. During that semester, one of my professors informed me of an aviation company that managed corporate pilots' flight schedules worldwide. He recommended that I apply for a job with the company. I took his advice and got hired. I took full-time classes in the evenings and worked full-time during the day.

While working for the aviation company, I realized that I wouldn't enjoy being a corporate pilot after all. I loved flying and I wanted to travel internationally, learning the cultures and customs of the world. I realized that if I flew for a company, I would be at my employer's beck and call 24 hours a day, constantly flying the same circuit of destinations.

Since I have so many other interests, I didn't know what I wanted to major in. I knew that I would have to carefully consider what I really wanted to pursue in order to obtain a bachelor's degree in a timely manner. I then decided that I would apply to my dream university.

Two years ago during the summer, I met and became friends with someone who worked for a commercial airline and offered me discount tickets to any destination in the world. Through those tickets, I took my first-ever international trip: I chose Germany because my first language is German, and I wanted to go to a country where I had the advantage of understanding people who couldn't speak English. After that, I flew regularly on my days off from work. Traveling exposed me to so many different cultures, landscapes, architecture, habits, philosophies, politics and religions. I was finally able to experience much of what I had only read and dreamed about since I was a little Amish girl.

Among the 20 countries I've been to thus far, my most enjoyable trips were going to India and Dubai, United Arab Emirates. In India I saw the Taj Mahal and many other beautiful architectural buildings and palaces. I also traveled up to the Himalayas where the Dalai Lama resides. In Dubai, I saw the world's tallest, first and only seven-star hotel shaped like a sailboat on a man-made island, an architectural wonder indeed. It was designed by a British architect Tom Wright and took five years to build to completion in 1999. The Dubai people have a host of other magnificent cutting-edge-technology buildings, such as the Emirates Airlines building that is shaped like an airplane.

In May last year, I quit my job at the aviation company. I needed a break to re-evaluate my goals for the future and since I felt drawn to the Dubai atmosphere, I spent two months there in the summer. While in Dubai, I learned of the Humanitad Foundation, a non-profit world peace organization based in London. Humanitad's celebrity campaign organizer introduced me to the foundation's mission and goals. I immediately knew that this was the perfect organization for me because it promoted tolerance and understanding towards all humankind with an entirely unbiased and nonpolitical approach. I met the founder in October, and he appointed me the art director for the organization, a position I accepted as a full-time volunteer to date. I work out of my home and communicate mostly via email with the founder regarding my project and Humanitad.

I am currently searching for and selecting one sculptor from each of the 192 nations in the world. The selected sculptor will create a sandstone block depicting his or her country's history, heritage, culture, mythology/religion and/or commerce. These blocks will then be built into a Peruvian-style stepped pyramid, possibly in Dubai in November. The Monument To Mankind will serve as a symbol of peaceful collaboration among all the nations in the world. It will also be the biggest international arts project in history.

We at Humanitad are planning to open an office in New York in January next year where I will be based. The ultimate goal for us is to achieve an agreement among all the nations for three days of world peace. We will celebrate this with 72 hours of nonstop musical events worldwide, hosted by several nations. New York will be the host location for America. In addition, all the three-day events will be broad-casted live on CNN with Hal Uplinger as our international broadcast production and syndication director. The Monument To Mankind will then be opened to the public and our child outreach, famine relief and educational programs, etc. will be in effect after that.

I plan on continuing my work with Humanitad as long as it does not take away from the time I need to focus 100 percent on my studies and successfully fulfill all that is required of me academically. I expect that I can only devote a small percentage of my time to Humanitad while I'm taking classes, but I plan on being part of the Humanitad core team long into the future.

I wish to pursue an architectural degree at Columbia University. My father used to co-design and build houses when I was still Amish. That is when I first became interested in houses and buildings. Because of that background, I have always consciously or sub-consciously appreciated well-designed architecture, but it was not until within the past year, after re-evaluating my life goals, that I concluded that it is indeed a field in which I would be able to excel and be happy. I am definitely artistically talented—I oil paint, draw, sing, etc.—and I believe that as long as I can utilize my creative flows and get the opportunities to travel frequently with constant exposure to all cultures, I will be satisfied. I believe that an architectural career will encourage my artistic abilities and open up opportunities to travel.

How To Interview Like A Pro

Acing The Admission Interview

It's one thing to express yourself on paper, but it's an entirely different ballgame when you do so in person. Some schools have the opportunity for you to do an in-person interview with an admission officer or an alumnus. If you can, you should take advantage of this opportunity. It is your chance to help your accomplishments shine brighter as well as to learn more about what the school has to offer you.

In addition to schools, many scholarship organizations request interviews as well. Selection committees use the interview as a way to get to know you beyond the application, and since it is frequently the last phase of the selection process, the interview is often very important. So good interview skills can help you get into and pay for college.

If the idea of doing an interview rattles your nerves, you're not alone. Many students get nervous in formal interview settings, knowing that the person on the other side of the table can determine where they spend the next two, four or more years of their studies. In this chapter, we cover some tips for calming your nerves as well as making the most of the time that you have.

The Two-Way Interview

If you're nervous about the interview, there's one thing that we would like you to know: You are not the only one under the gun. Your interviewer is as well. You see, interviewers are not only trying to learn about you and what you have to bring to their school. They are also trying to get you excited about attending their school. In other words, they are trying to impress you as much as you are trying to impress them.

Surprised?

Keep this thought in mind as you are approaching an interview to calm your nerves. It's a different way of looking at the interview and takes some pressure off of you to know that the interviewer is as much being interviewed as you are.

Questions To Expect

Another reason not to get nervous about interviews is that there will probably be no surprise questions. Schools basically want to know about your academic preparedness for the program, your fit with their school and what special skills, talents or experiences you may bring to their student body. Knowing this, you can probably guess many of the questions you will be asked.

To take all of the guesswork out of the equation, here are some typical questions:

- Why do you want to attend this school?
- What are you looking for in a college or graduate school?
- What would you like to study and why?
- What are your plans after graduation?
- How does this degree fit into your long-term career plans?
- What are your long-term career plans?
- What work, academic or other experiences have prepared you for returning to school?
- What do you do outside of work?
- What have you been doing since you were last in school?
- What made you decide to return to school?

As you can see, there are no real surprises with these questions which means that you can stop the hand-wringing over questions you don't know how to answer.

Practice For The Real Thing

If you've ever played a musical instrument, performed or given a speech, then you know that the best way to do well is to practice. The same is true for interviewing. If you want to do well in the interview, you need to practice.

Ask a friend or family member to sit down with you for a mock interview. Give them a list of questions, let them know the purpose of the interview and then have them fire away. Ask them to take note not only of your answers but also how you answer the questions. Are you comfortable? Fidgeting? Making eye contact?

As you are doing the mock interview, answer questions as you would in a real interview. When you are finished, listen to their feedback and then use the feedback to help you the next time around.

By practicing, you will get more comfortable answering questions about yourself and your goals and you'll perform much better during the real thing.

Do Your Homework On The School

One of the biggest pet peeves of interviewers is students who know absolutely nothing about their schools. Unfortunately, this happens more often that you might imagine. Students have been known to ask what majors are offered and even where a school is located, questions that are easily answered with a little bit of research beforehand.

You don't need to know everything about a school before heading into an interview, but it helps to know something about it. It will make you look better prepared and more serious about attending the school.

You can learn about the school by reading its literature from brochures and on its website, by speaking with students or recent alumni or by visiting the campus. Knowing what you like about the school's academic and social offerings will help you answer questions about why you want to attend the school and what you are looking for in a college or graduate school.

Have A Conversation, Not Interrogation

It's important to remember that an interview is not like a police interrogation. You are not there just to answer the questions fired at you. Rather, you want to create a two-way dialogue or conversation with your interviewer. This will make the conversation more interesting for both you and your interviewer.

You can do this by asking questions about the school and your interviewer. You can also comment on remarks that they make. For example, if you speak about your desire to study business, and your interviewer mentions that the school has strong relationships with local businesses to give students hands-on experience, you can ask for more information about these relationships.

By doing this, you demonstrate that you are not just at the interview to speak about yourself but also that you are listening and learning about the school as well. Interviewers appreciate this attentiveness and will thank you for creating such a memorable conversation.

Have An Inquiring Mind

One of the best ways to show your interest in a school is by asking questions. Doing this shows your interviewers that you've spent some time studying up on their school to be able to formulate the questions and that you are interested enough to want to learn more.

The secret to asking questions is that you can develop a list of them beforehand. You don't need to memorize your list of questions or think of them on the spot. In fact, the best questions you can ask are probably the ones that develop over time.

The key is to ask questions that don't have obvious answers or answers that could easily be found in the school's brochure or on its website. Instead, ask your interviewers for their opinions, about the advantages or disadvantages of a program or about something without a straight yes or no answer.

To get you started, here are some questions you could ask:

■ What kind of academic support do you provide for adult students? Career counseling support? Social support?

■ What are some typical career paths for students who study xyz major?

■ What kind of services does your adult services office provide?

■ Can you tell me about the adult student community at your school?

■ How strong is your alumni network?

■ What do you think that your school offers that I might not get from another school?

Questions like these require opinions and are not easily answered in the school's brochures or on its website.

The Scholarship Interview

Many scholarship organizations have interviews so that the selection committee can get to know you beyond words on paper in the application. There are some similarities between admission interviews and scholarship interviews. For example, it is still helpful to practice interviewing to ease you into the process. You should still do your homework, although this time it is on the awarding organization. You should know something about what the organization is trying to achieve and why it is giving the scholarship away. And, you should try to create a two-way conversation rather than an interrogation to keep the attention of the selection committee.

One of the main differences is the purpose of the two kinds of interviews. With a scholarship interview, there is a single purpose or goal that the awarding organization is trying to achieve. You must figure out what this is. Fortunately, it's usually not difficult. You can find it in the description of the scholarship. For example, a community organization may want to give its scholarship to a local student who has overcome difficulties to pursue an education, a hospital may want to reward future health care professionals or a library may want to support future librarians.

It's important to understand why the organization is awarding the scholarship so that you can figure out which of your experiences to share to illustrate how you are the best fit for the student they are seeking. If you were applying for an award for students who have overcome difficulties, you would want to describe which challenges you've faced and how you've worked to overcome them. Similarly, if you were applying for the librarian scholarship, you would need to explain why your future goal is to become a librarian and how you are fit to do so.

It's important to think about what the scholarship organization is trying to achieve because the interview is often the last step in the selection process. This means that you must make the strongest impression possible because hundreds or thousands of dollars may hang in the balance.

Don't Let Your Nerves Get The Best Of You

Throughout the interview process, you want to be yourself. Remember that the interview itself will most likely not make or break your chances of getting into a college or graduate school. It is one factor that the school will consider, but your fate does not rest entirely in your interviewers' hands.

You will perform your best if you've spent some time to practice and learn about the school and then just be yourself during the real thing.

How To Get The Best Recommendations

How To Get The Best Recommendations

Colleges and graduate schools often want to know want others think of you. This is where the recommendation comes in. Recommendations give them feedback from others who know you and who can vouch for your background and abilities.

Some schools request one or two recommendations, and some scholarship organizations request them as well. Typically these are from previous employers, teachers or professors. Your recommenders will write about your career or academic abilities, character and preparedness for your studies.

Schools and scholarship organizations use recommendation letters as a way of rounding out their picture of you. Your recommenders may offer additional insight from their perspective. They can also verify what you have written in your applications and essays.

In this chapter, we'll help you make sure that you select the right people to ask for recommendations and that you provide them with everything that they need to write about you. While recommendation letters will not by themselves make or break your chances of admission or of winning a scholarship, you certainly want them to help rather than hinder.

Who To Ask

Almost every admission officer can remember a student who has unknowingly submitted recommendation letters that were not positive. The mistake that these students made is that they asked the wrong person to write their letters, something that you can easily avoid with a little bit of forethought.

Depending on how long the break has been since you were last in school and how much you have maintained contact with them, you may want to ask a former teacher or professor to write a recommendation. The key is that you'll want to select a teacher or professor who knows you well not only as a student but as a person.

In other words, don't select a teacher or professor just because you got a good grade in their class. Select one in whose class you actively participated, with whom you talked outside of class or who knows something about you besides your grades on an exam. Ideally, you can select someone with whom you have both an educational and personal relationship.

If you have not been in school recently, you'll probably want to select a previous employer or manager. Try to select someone who has seen firsthand the quality of the work that you do, who has seen you take initiative or show leadership and who understands how going back to school fits your career goals. The more your manager can say about your accomplishments, how well you work with others or how diligent you are the better.

A lot of students make the mistake of asking someone they think has high name recognition rather than someone who knows them well. For example, students may ask the president of the company or a city council member for a recommendation when they have barely met them in passing. More important than the title of your recommenders is what they say about you.

It's also important that you find people who you know have good things to say about you. If you ask them to write a recommendation and they hesitate or give you a reason why they might not be the best person to write the letter, this is an immediate signal that you need to ask somebody else. It may seem self-evident, but many students don't take these warning signals and end up with mediocre or even negative recommendation letters.

How To Help Your Recommenders

We are always looking for ways to make our lives easier, simpler and more efficient. This is exactly the gift that you can give your recommenders by providing them with all of the materials and background information that they'll need to write your recommendations. Doing so will make their job easier, reflect well on your organizational skills and help them write strong recommendations.

Here are the things that you should provide:

Cover letter. A cover letter thanks them in advance for their help with the recommendations, lets them know your goals for applying to the schools, provides the schools and their deadlines and gives instructions for what they should do with the completed recommendations. You can even remind them of some of your more outstanding accomplishments that you think would fit nicely into your recommendations. These are especially good to mention if they are accomplishments with which your recommenders are familiar.

Forms and stamped, pre-addressed envelopes. They'll have all of the materials in one place as well as know where to send the forms once they complete them.

Resume. This will help remind them of your experiences and accomplishments that they may include in your recommendations. Refer to Chapter 5 for tips on how to put together your resume. You'll want to make sure that you not just list your accomplishments but that you also describe the effects of them. In other words, don't just say that you were a member of an organization, but describe your role, any leadership positions you held and what you accomplished as a member.

By doing all of the legwork for your recommenders, you'll make sure that they have everything they need to write stellar recommendations.

TEN

Earn Credits Outside Of The Classroom

Earn Credits Outside Of The Classroom

While it might seem impossible to put a price on education, colleges have found a way to do so through the "credit" system. Basically, each class is assigned a certain number of credits based on the difficulty level and/or time commitment. Each credit costs a set amount, and it takes a specific number of credits to graduate. Therefore, the more credits you take the more money you'll have to pay.

But what if you could earn some credits for free? Not only would it shorten the amount of time that you had to spend in school, but it would also save you a bundle of money.

There are several ways that you may be able to earn credits for free. The most common is if you have already taken some college-level courses. With your transcript, you may be able to use these courses to count toward your degree. Of course, if you took these courses a long time ago in subject areas that rapidly change, the credits may not count but it certainly is worth asking.

Another way you can earn credit is to show the college that specific life experiences and training you have received while working are equivalent to college credit. You may not realize it but you have amassed a variety of skills through your life, and some of these can be converted into credit that counts toward your degree.

Some colleges even offer ways to earn more credits than normal through accelerated programs. Also, if your college does not charge based on classes but instead has a set fee per semester then if you load up on extra classes you are effectively getting those courses and credits for free. Of course, you'll work a lot harder, too!

Earn College Credit Through Exams

By passing certain exams you can prove to the college that you know the material and therefore receive credit. There are several exams that are popular, however, you should check with your school to make sure they will accept the scores. The following are the most common exams that adults use to get college credit:

College Level Examination Program. Your college may let you take CLEP exams to receive college credit. There are currently 2,900 colleges that give credit or advanced standing to students who pass CLEP exams. There are two types of CLEP exams. One is a general subject exam that covers math, English, humanities, natural science and social science and history. The other is a subject exam that covers a specific course. A passing score in this exam will usually give you credit for that specific course. There are currently 30 subject exams. A CLEP exam costs $50 to take but could save you thousands of dollars in tuition. Plus, you don't want to take a course in an area in which you are already proficient. Get more information at www. collegeboard.com.

The DSST Exam. Originally designed for the military, the DANTES Subject Standardized Tests (DSST) may now be taken by anyone. More than 80,000 people take the DSST each year to receive college credit. By passing the DSST exam, you can earn credit for what you already know and thus save money. Get more details at www.dantes.doded.mil.

Excelsior College Examinations. There are 40 undergraduate-level Excelsior College Examinations that are accepted at nearly 900 colleges and universities. The undergraduate-level Excelsior College Examinations (as well as the DSST and CLEP exams) are free to military personnel. Those not affiliated with the military may request fee information. Get more information at www.excelsior. edu/exams/.

Graduate Record Exam. While the GRE is usually for graduate school admission, some colleges allow undergraduates to earn credits with GRE scores. Check with your department to see if GRE scores can be used to satisfy specific course requirements. Get more information at www.ets.org/tests.html.

Job Ready Assessment Tests. There are 75 Job Ready Assessment tests that you can take to get credit in vocational or technical fields. Exams include tests in accounting, computer programming, construction, drafting, plumbing, welding and more. Get more information at www.nocti.org.

Get Credit For Life Experience

As an adult student you might be able to get college credit for your professional and life experiences. Most schools recognize that you can gain college-level knowledge through your own life experiences. If your experiences are general and not related to a specific course, you might obtain general studies credit. Or, you may get credit for specific courses if you have had related experiences or training.

In the book *College Degrees By Mail* there are examples of ways that colleges may recognize life experiences. For example:

- Work can demonstrate such skills as typing, filing, inventory control, accounting, computer programming, welding, editing and sales.

- Homemaking can show your proficiency in home maintenance, household planning and budgeting, childcare, meal planning and nutrition and child psychology.

- Volunteer work can show experience with community service, political campaigns, church activities and service organizations.

The first thing you should do is contact your department or admission office to see what experiences qualify and what kind of substantiation you need to provide.

The Learning Portfolio Evaluation

Often to receive college credit for your life experiences or previous studies, colleges want proof. You can provide this with a learning portfolio. In the portfolio you give a self-assessment, detailing the type of learning or training you have received outside of the classroom. Usually you will write a main essay and provide supporting documents. You want to make a case for how this learning is comparable to college-level learning and prove to the college that you possess the knowledge within this field.

A typical portfolio may include:

- Your work history along with any volunteer experiences

- Formal educational experiences and special training

- Specific recognition for your knowledge including any licenses

- Hobbies and interests

- Meaningful life experiences

- Specific knowledge and skills gained

The key is to not make a laundry list of everything that you have done but instead to explain what you have learned and how it applies to your field of study. Be analytical about what you have gained from the experience, and demonstrate that this learning is equivalent to what you would learn in college. Look at the course catalog and match your knowledge to specific courses. You also need to show that you understand the theories behind your knowledge. In other words, just because you can drive a boat does not mean you understand the theory behind hydrodynamics. It will help if you speak to a member of your department to get the specific details on what your portfolio should look like.

Earn Credit By Credential Evaluation

Credit by evaluation is when a college looks at any education or training that you have received and determines if it is equal to a course offered by the college. This may include traditional classes at colleges or course work and training while in the military, while working or in schools that are not accredited or in organizations that are not primarily educational institutions. Speak to your department to request credit by evaluation. Most schools use the *National Guide to Educational Credit for Training Programs*, the *Guide to Educational*

Credit by Examination and the *Guide to the Evaluation of Educational Experiences in the Armed Services* published by the American Council on Education.

Many colleges also offer a proficiency or challenge exam. As the name suggests, these exams let you prove that you have the knowledge or experience necessary to pass a specific course. It's like passing the final exam of a course without having actually taken the class. Speak to your professor or department head to see if an exam is an option at your school.

Paying For College As An Adult Student

How To Pay For Your Education

G etting into college is one thing. Finding the money to pay for tuition is something else entirely. Unfortunately, many adults simply don't take advantage of all of the opportunities that are out there to help them pay for school. We wrote an entire book, *501 Ways For Adult Students to Pay For College*, that we highly recommend you read to learn how to make your education affordable. In this chapter we'll summarize a few of the more important ways that you can pay for college. This should be your starting point. Make sure you thoroughly investigate each of these areas.

Getting Your Share Of Federal Financial Aid

Each year more than $134 billion is awarded in financial aid. With this much money being paid out, you definitely need to make sure that you get every penny that you deserve. Unfortunately, the biggest mistake that most adults make is not applying for financial aid because they assume that they won't qualify. Some adults even assume that financial aid is only for high school students! As long as you are working toward your first undergraduate or graduate degree, you can apply for financial aid regardless of your age.

Some adults assume that their family income may be too high to qualify for financial aid. The reality is you'll never know what you truly deserve unless you apply. You may find that even if you don't get a grant, you are awarded a cushy campus job, special college scholarships or low-interest student loans. You may find that one of these sources of money is just what you need to make paying for college possible. We cannot emphasize how important it is that you spend the time to apply for financial aid.

Starting The Financial Aid Process

The financial aid process begins by providing detailed information on your personal finances through a form known as the Free Application for Federal Student Aid or FAFSA. Using your previous year's taxes you will reveal all of the money that you have in savings, investments and hidden Swiss bank accounts. If you are applying to a private college you may also have to provide additional information through the college's own financial aid form or the College Board's CSS/Financial Aid PROFILE form. Like the FAFSA, it asks similar questions about your finances.

You may download a copy of these forms and even complete them online at www.fafsa.ed.gov for the FAFSA and www. collegeboard.com for the PROFILE.

You can turn in both the FAFSA and PROFILE as soon as possible after January 1 of the year in which you plan to go back to school. If you are planning on starting in September 2008, turn in your FAFSA as soon after January 1, 2008 as possible. The reason you can't turn the forms in earlier is because you need to know your prior year's income and assets. You should turn in your applications as early as possible since each college has its own deadlines, which are usually in early to mid-February. Most colleges award financial aid until they run out of money. This somewhat first come, first served process means that the earlier you turn in your forms the better.

Here's what happens. First, you submit the FAFSA to the government for processing. The government will in turn pass on the results of their calculations to you in the form of the Student Aid Report (SAR) as well as to each college that you are applying to. The SAR provides your Expected Family Contribution (EFC), the amount that you are personally expected to contribute to your education. It is important to understand that all the government does is crunch the numbers you provide on the FAFSA and pass the results to the colleges. This means that you need to indicate on the FAFSA which colleges should receive the results.

We want to point out that you are filling out your financial aid forms nearly seven months before you start school and using tax returns that will be a year old. This is an important point to keep in mind since anything that happens to your finances now won't affect your financial aid situation. In other words, your financial aid package for the upcoming school year is really based on information from last tax year. Everything that happens to you financially after the new year won't even be seen by the colleges when it comes to your financial aid forms.

What Happens After The Numbers Are Crunched

While applying for financial aid may seem like putting the fate of your future into a computer that crunches the numbers and spits out an answer, there is actually a human being behind all financial aid decisions. Once your financial aid forms have been processed, they will be sent to every college you are applying to, and this is where the computations end and human beings take over.

With a detailed picture of your financial situation, financial aid officers at each of the colleges will analyze the money you have and figure out your degree of financial need based on the cost of the college. Once they know how much you need, they put together a financial aid package, spelling out how much and in what form you will get this money.

Financial aid officers use the results as a guide when putting together your aid package. The financial aid officer has the ability to increase or decrease the amount of financial aid you receive for a variety of reasons. Therefore, it is crucial that you are open about your family's true financial situation to the financial aid officer. Remember, too, that all financial aid is based on your previous year's taxes. A lot may have happened this year that is not reflected by last year's taxes.

If you want to share additional information, you can send a letter to the college financial aid office to explain any unusual circumstances that may affect your family's finances. Most colleges include a space on their financial aid forms for you to describe any relevant information. When you are thinking about writing this letter, consider the following three points.

Don't hide the dirty laundry. Most people when filling out financial forms feel compelled to hide embarrassing circumstances.

After all you are revealing your financial strengths and weaknesses to a total stranger. However, if you have extraordinary circumstances such as large medical bills, unemployment, recent or ongoing divorce, supporting extended family members or any additional expenses that may not be reflected in your FAFSA or PROFILE, tell the financial aid officer. Don't be embarrassed. It could cost you big time.

Give the college a reason to give you more money. Financial aid officers are numbers people. However, they have wide latitude for interpreting numbers and may apply a variety of standards and make exceptions, which can help or hurt your case. To get the most support from these professionals, make your case with numbers. You can't just say that you don't have enough money. You need to show it. Document with numbers why your tax forms don't accurately reflect your true income or expenses.

Don't try to trick the college. The human being in the financial aid process is also what keeps it safe from trickery. You could, for example, take all of the money in your savings account and plunk it down to buy an around-the-world vacation. On paper you have no savings. Yet, when the financial aid officer looks at your income, he or she will think it is very odd that someone who earns a decent living and owns a nice house is so cash poor. This is a red flag, and you'll be asked to provide additional information. Once the financial aid officer learns how you spent your savings, not only would he or she not give you more financial aid but you would also have no money left to pay for college even if you wanted to.

Financial aid officers are experts at reading financial statements. Just by looking at your 1099 interest statements they can get an estimate of the size of your assets. Trying to trick the college or not report certain income or assets will only backfire. Financial aid officers are professionals who have seen every trick in the book. Our best advice on trickery is to not attempt it.

What You Can Expect From Financial Aid

The way in which your aid is packaged will differ not only because your financial need changes with the price of each college but also because colleges have varying amounts of financial aid resources. The following is a detailed description of what you might find in your aid package. Most financial aid packages consist of a combination of these sources.

Federal Pell Grants. These grants are for undergraduate study for students who have the most financial need, typically with Expected Family Contributions of $3,800 or less. The amount varies based on your EFC, but the maximum amount for the 2007-08 school year is $4,310. All students who apply for financial aid by completing the FAFSA and are determined to have financial need by their college will be considered for Federal Pell Grants.

Federal Supplemental Educational Opportunity Grants. These grants are for undergraduates with the most financial need. The government provides limited funds for individual schools to administer this program. This means there is no guarantee that every eligible student will receive an FSEOG Grant. The amount varies between $100 and $4,000 per year, and the specific amount is determined by the college on a case-by-case basis.

Grants from the college. The college itself has various need- and merit-based grants. By applying for financial aid you will be considered for these grants. Many schools also have grants reserved just for adult students.

State grants. Your state may offer both need- and merit-based grants. While some grants are administered by the state, others are distributed to the colleges to administer.

Federal Work-Study. Work-study provides jobs for undergraduate and graduate students with financial need allowing you to earn money while attending school. The focus is on providing work experience in your area of study. Generally, you will work for your school on campus or for a nonprofit organization or public agency if you work off campus. You will have a limit on the hours you can work in this program. Your wages are based on the federal minimum wage although they are usually higher.

State Work-Study. Besides the federal program, some states also have a work-study program that mirrors the operation of the federal program.

Federal Perkins Loans. Federal Perkins Loans are low-interest loans for undergraduate and graduate students with extreme financial need. Your school provides the loan from governmental as well as its own funds. You may borrow up to $4,000 per year as an under-graduate or $6,000 per year as a graduate student. The interest rate is fixed at 5 percent and there are no additional fees.

Subsidized and Unsubsidized Federal Stafford Loans. There are two types of Stafford Loans: Direct Stafford Loans and FFEL Stafford Loans. For Direct Stafford Loans, the U.S. government is the lender. For FFEL Stafford Loans, the lender is a participating bank, credit union or other lender, which you can locate by contacting your school. You may borrow up to $3,500 as a freshman, $4,500 as a sophomore and $5,500 as a junior or senior undergraduate student. Graduate students may borrow through the **PLUS Loans for Graduate and Professional Degree Students**.

Remember, you are free to pick and choose from your financial aid offer. When you receive an offer of financial aid you don't have to accept or reject the whole package. For example, if you are offered a grant you'll definitely want to accept it, but you might not want to accept the loan component.

Tips For Maximizing Your Financial Aid

Colleges run out of money so turn in applications early. The deadlines for turning in your financial aid applications vary by college. You want to turn in your FAFSA as soon as possible after January 1. The reason is that colleges have a limited amount of financial aid. If you turn in your applications late, even if you deserve aid, you may not get it simply because the college ran out of money.

Use estimates if you haven't finished your taxes. To complete your financial aid forms you need to provide information from your tax forms. Since taxes are not due until April 15 and many people wait until April 14 to do them, it is not surprising that many students wait until they get their taxes done before filling out the financial aid forms. This is a huge mistake since it could mean turning in your financial aid forms past the college's deadline. Use estimates on your financial aid forms since you can always revise those numbers with actual numbers once you finish your taxes. Better yet do your taxes early this year. It's much cleaner to use real numbers so that there won't be any surprises.

Think about financial aid early–at least a year before you start school. Remember that all of the numbers used in financial calculations come from the previous tax year. If you are starting college in September 2008, then your tax return from 2007 will be the basis for that first year. Therefore, if you wait until January 2008 to think about financial aid, it will be too late to do anything that will affect the outcome of your first year. (Of course, you could still do things to affect your financial aid for your second year in school.)

You must apply for financial aid every year. Financial aid is determined on a year-by-year basis. That means that even if you didn't get financial aid this year you should apply next year since your finances will have changed, especially after paying for one year of tuition. Some students find that after the first or second year of college they have reduced their income and assets to the point where they qualify for financial aid. There is a Renewal FAFSA that you may use, which saves a lot of time when applying for aid the next year.

If you need more, don't be shy about asking for a re-evaluation. If you feel that the amount of financial aid that you are offered by a college is simply nowhere near enough, you can ask for a re-evaluation. For the re-evaluation to be effective you need to provide the financial aid office with concrete reasons why their initial assessment was wrong. Start with a letter or call to the financial aid office. Be sure that you have all of your documents ready, and remember that the squeaky wheel gets the grease. If you don't say anything about your package, the college will assume that you are happy with it.

Get more help with the FAFSA. If you need help completing the FAFSA, visit the U.S. Department of Education website at www.fafsa.ed.gov or call 800-4-FED-AID. The website will take you step by step through the entire process. You may also want to contact the financial aid offices at a few local colleges since many hold free workshops to help students complete the FAFSA.

Scholarships For Adult Students

Contrary to popular belief there are scholarships for adult students. To find scholarships that you have the best chance of winning, you are going to need to do some detective work. There are no shortcuts. But by doing so you will be able to not only find more awards but also awards that really fit your background and goals, which will dramatically increase your odds of winning.

As an adult you'll find that there are two major types of scholarships. The first are scholarships specifically for adult students. There are a number of scholarships for "non-traditional" or "returning" students. These have specific requirements that exclude "traditional" students such as an age minimum or requiring that applicants have taken a break from school to raise a family or work. The second are scholarships aimed at any student who is in college regardless of whether they are "traditional" or "adult." These scholarships are far more numerous and usually require that you are in a specific year of study such as a freshman in college or that you pursue a particular major. Scholarships that are open to college freshmen are also the ones that you'll apply to before you actually start school. Most of these scholarships let you apply before you actually begin so that you can use the money to pay for your first year in school. These scholarships typically don't have an age limit, which means that you will compete against not only other adult students but also traditional students.

It's this second type of scholarship that most adults don't consider because they are not specifically directed at adult students. But if you ignore these you will be leaving a ton of money on the table. The golden rule of scholarships is: Unless a scholarship specifically says that you need to be a high school student to apply then you should feel free to apply for it as long as it matches your interests and goals. Remember, a college freshman can be 17 years old or 70 years old. It doesn't make a difference for these scholarships. Consider every scholarship that does not explicitly exclude you as fair game.

Now let's roll up our sleeves and find some scholarships.

The Internet

The Internet puts the world's biggest library at your fingertips and allows you access to an unprecedented amount of information. It can also be truly frustrating. The problem with searching for scholarships online is that there is no filtering. Type in the word "scholarship" into a search engine, and you'll get more than 5,000,000 results. Only a fraction of these results will actually be useful to you. To solve this problem of too much information, there are specialized websites that let you search databases of scholarships. For the best of these, you fill out some information about yourself and with the click of a mouse are matched to scholarships that you may apply to win.

Sound too easy? In some ways it is. Don't rely on these websites to find every scholarship that's right for you. Many students make the mistake of assuming that once they do an Internet search they have exhausted all sources for scholarships. The reality is that no matter how many scholarships these websites claim to have in their database none of them even comes close to the total number of scholarships that are available. Plus, none of these websites do a good job of listing local scholarship opportunities—which in many ways offer you some of the best chances to get free cash for college.

So without further ado here are some good places to start. Remember, these websites are just the beginning of your search for free cash for college.

- **SuperCollege** (www.supercollege.com)
- **CollegeAnswer** (www.collegeanswer.com)

- **BrokeScholar** (www.brokescholar.com)

- **Free Scholarship Information** (www.freschinfo.com)

- **The College Board** (www.collegeboard.com)

- **The Princeton Review** (www.review.com)

- **FinancialAid.com** (www.financialaid.com)

- **FastAid** (www.fastaid.org)

- **Scholarships.com** (www.scholarships.com)

- **Petersons** (www.petersons.com)

- **CollegeNet** (www.collegenet.com)

Scholarship Books

Even though they lack the pizzazz of the Internet, scholarship books should not be overlooked. A good book provides a huge number of awards and an index to help you find the ones that match your achievements and background.

One that we recommend, and it is not an impartial opinion by any means, is our book, *501 Ways For Adult Students to Pay For College*. This is the only book that we are aware of that addresses the specific needs of adult students to pay for college. In this book, you'll learn how to find the best scholarships for adult students, get your employer to pay for your education, earn college credits for lifetime and work experiences, take advantage of federal and state retraining programs and more. Also consider *Get Free Cash For College*. We wrote this book after getting frustrated with many traditional scholarship books that cost too much and gave too little. We wanted to write a book that listed awards that most students could win. We also wanted to make sure that we didn't just give you the scholarships to apply to but that we also showed you how to win. Regardless of whether you read our books, you should not ignore the value of traditional scholarship books and directories. They are a great source of awards as well as tips on how to win.

Community Service Organizations

Every city or town has various civic groups and public service organizations. Many of these groups spend the year fundraising to be able to award scholarships. While some may direct their awards through the local high school, you'll find others have awards open to future college students of any age.

There are also an increasing number of civic groups that are creating dedicated adult student scholarships. For example, the Chagrin Valley Junior Women's Club in Ohio offers a $1,000 scholarship to an adult female over the age of 25 who wants to return for an undergraduate education. Many local Rotary Clubs, which have long sponsored awards for high school seniors, are establishing similar awards for adult students. Since these scholarships are limited only to those who live in the community that the club serves, there are no national directories or lists of these scholarships. Even on the Internet there are no websites that offer a comprehensive list of local scholarships. Plus, new scholarships are constantly being created so any directory that you find is out of date from the first day it is published.

The best way to track down these awards is to get out your phone book and make a list of the service clubs in your community. While you're at it, why not dial the number and ask if they offer a scholarship? Keep in mind that most service clubs also belong to a national organization. Both the local and the national organization may offer their own scholarships.

In addition to the phone book, visit your community center. The people who work there should know the names of most of the service clubs in your community. Your local public librarian can also help you track down these organizations.

To make sure you haven't missed any groups, get in your car and drive to the city limit. Usually on the same sign that welcomes visitors to your city is a modern day totem pole with the plaques of the various civic groups that are active in your community.

Non-Profit Organizations And Charities

One of the growing sources of scholarship dollars is from local charities and non-profit foundations. These organizations often raise money for specific causes, and education is usually one of them. Many of the scholarships given by charities are aimed at students who otherwise could not afford to go back to school. Another common focus of these organizations is to help adults pay for training in specific vocational skills to help them re-enter the workforce or advance their careers.

For example, the Midland Area Foundation in Michigan (www.midlandfoundation.com) offers the Dr. Shailer L. Bass Memorial Scholarship for non-traditional students. This $2,000 award is for Midland County adults pursuing post-high school studies at a college or university.

Similarly the San Diego Foundation (www.sdfoundation.org) administers a variety of scholarships for its residents including the Dorothy M. Bolyard Memorial Scholarship, which is open to residents over the age of 24 who are pursuing a degree at a two- or four-year university in San Diego County. The foundation also offers the Herman H. Derksen Scholarship, which is open to any resident who is pursuing a trade or vocational program. If you visit the website of the San Diego Foundation you'll find that the adult student scholarships are mixed in with the high school student scholarships. In fact, to apply for one of the adult scholarships you use the same application that high school students use for their awards. This underscores the importance of being thorough in your research and to not assume that just because a foundation sponsors a lot of scholarships for high school students that it doesn't also have some for adult students.

To find the charities and foundations in your area, visit your local public library and ask the reference librarian for a directory of local charities and foundations. Also, every time you speak to a charity to ask about scholarships, make sure you also ask if they know of other groups that you may contact.

Professional Associations

Whether you want to be a computer scientist or certified fraud examiner there is a professional organization to support your profession. In fact, in the U.S. alone there are more than 135,000 professional associations. One of the missions of these organizations is to support students who want to enter the field. Many of them accomplish this by offering scholarships.

In our scholarship book, *Get Free Cash For College*, we list many of the best professional organizations that offer scholarships. We recommend that you look at *Get Free Cash For College* as well as another book called the *Encyclopedia of Associations* published by the Gale Group. This is a multi-volume set that is extremely expensive to buy. Fortunately, you can find this book at most college libraries. Inside you will find a detailed list of nearly every association in the country.

Another way to find professional associations is to talk to the people who are already in these careers. If you're studying to be a dental assistant, spend some time talking to dental assistants and learn which associations they belong to. You can also go to the library and read the trade journals for the profession. Associations often advertise in these publications.

Once you've found professional associations for your career field, contact them to see if they offer awards. If they don't, they may be able to direct you to other groups that do.

Unions

If you belong to a union or plan to enter a field that has one, be sure to check with the union for any potential scholarships. Many unions offer education benefits to their members. The American Federation of Labor-Congress of Industrial Organizations (AFL-CIO), which has 64 member unions, maintains a nice directory of scholarships. In fact, their directory lists over $4 million in union-sponsored scholarships. You can search their list at www.aflcio.org. If your union is not a part of the AFL-CIO, then go directly to your union representative and ask about their educational benefits.

Local Businesses—Big And Small

As a way to say "thank you" to customers, many businesses offer scholarships for students in their community. Take a look at all of the retail businesses, services and any corporate home offices that are in your area. The supermarket chain Fred Meyer, for example, offers scholarships through Portland State University to undergraduate students. In San Diego, Anheuser-Busch sponsors the Eagle Achievement-Adult Scholarship through the League of United Latin American Citizens.

To find businesses in your area, check with your local chamber of commerce. You can visit the national chamber of commerce online at www.uschamber.com and from there you can find your local chamber. Most chambers maintain a directory of member companies that you can view. Be sure to ask the people who work at the chamber if they are aware of any companies that award scholarships.

Whenever you are shopping, be on the lookout for awards. Many students have stumbled across scholarships by picking up a brochure at the cash register. If your city is the headquarters for any large company, investigate if that company offers a scholarship.

Most large companies offer scholarships through their own foundations. For example, Wal-Mart has the Sam Walton Foundation, while Bank of America has the Bank of America Foundation. These foundations are separate entities, and you need to speak to someone who works for the foundation (not the company) to find out what specific scholarships may be available.

Beyond Financial Aid And Scholarships

In addition to financial aid and scholarships, many students also turn to other sources of money such as student loans. Going to college is an investment in yourself, and often you will need to borrow some money to pay for this investment. Fortunately, there are many places that are willing to lend you money, often on very generous terms. We'll begin by looking at traditional student loans and then investigate a few lesser-known places to borrow money.

Student Loans

For most, a student loan will be the best and cheapest way to borrow money—unless of course you have the option of an interest-free loan from rich Aunt Emma. Since that's not an option for most, to qualify for a student loan you need to apply for financial aid by filling out the Free Application for Federal Student Aid (FAFSA). When you submit the FAFSA, you not only check if you qualify for grant money, but you also establish your eligibility to receive government-backed, low-interest loans.

There are two types of student loans: subsidized and unsubsidized. For subsidized loans, the government pays the interest on your loan while you are in school so that interest doesn't accrue during that time. For unsubsidized loans, interest accrues while you are in school and you'll end up paying that interest once you start repayment. Whether a loan is subsidized or unsubsidized does not affect when you need to start paying back your loans, it only affects how much interest accrues while you are in school.

If you need to take out a student loan, the biggest choice you'll have to make is from whom to borrow the money. In fact, you'll probably find that you have a bunch of banks lining up to offer you money. While money is the same regardless of which bank you choose, you want to be a smart shopper by taking advantage of what are known as "borrower benefits."

As a loan borrower you can get valuable benefits for choosing one bank over another. Often these benefits are money-saving incentives for things such as making on-time payments, making payments via auto-debit or signing up for other services provided by the bank or loan servicer. These incentives may come in the form of partial interest rate reductions or even reductions to the principal balance of your outstanding loans. Usually, you won't need to change anything about the way you repay your loans when an incentive is applied to your account. The monthly payment amount remains the same, and you save money by repaying your loan balance more quickly.

So when you are trying to decide where to get your loan from, compare borrower benefits and then choose the loan that gives you the best benefits.

Private Loans

Not all student loans are government-backed students loans. In fact, you might find that private loans meet your needs. There are also loans that are not specifically designed to pay for college but that still make a lot of sense to use. Many banks and financial institutions offer special loans for students. These typically mirror the federal student loans. However, since they are private loans and not guaranteed by the government, their terms are set by the individual lenders. These loans can be extremely useful if you exhaust your federal sources of aid. Plus, since they are private loans you may apply for them at any time during the school year.

You apply for these loans directly with your lender. The interest rate will often be based on your credit history. The better your credit the lower your interest rate. Most private loans allow you to defer your interest and principal payments until after you graduate. When selecting a private loan, compare the interest rates, repayment options, loan terms and borrower benefits.

Another option is if you own your home you may be able to use your home's equity to pay for college. Basically, a home equity loan allows you to use the equity in your home as collateral. You can borrow a lump sum and make monthly payments or you can establish a line of credit and borrow money as you need it.

When you establish a line of credit you only pay the interest on the amount of money that you actually borrow. Interest rates can either be fixed or variable depending on the loan.

Home equity loans have some major advantages over other types of consumer borrowing. For one, you can deduct interest from your taxes. Even more important may be the fact that borrowing what you need when you need it will not impact your assets as much as taking it all in one lump sum. This means that a home equity line of credit should have less of an impact on your ability to get financial aid. The lower impact that a home equity line of credit has on your assets combined with the tax deduction you get for interest paid makes this one of the better private loans to use to pay for college.

You can also make withdrawals from traditional IRAs, Roth IRAs and SIMPLE IRAs and avoid the 10 percent early withdrawal penalty if you use the funds for qualified educational expenses. You will still have to pay income tax on the amount. If you can stomach the risk, you can borrow money from your 401k plan. You will need to repay yourself the principal and interest within a five-year period. The risk is that if you lose your job you will have to repay the loan immediately or else face the double whammy of income tax and a penalty on the amount you borrowed.

Money From Your State

You may not like it when every time you buy something the state tacks on an extra 4 to 8 percent in sales tax. But you can take some consolation in the fact that you may get back some of these dollars through financial aid programs offered by your state. Every state has an agency or department that helps students pay for college. Many states also administer their own centralized financial aid and scholarship programs. Your state agency is a clearinghouse not only for information but also for actual dollars for college.

Your first step is to find your state agency from the list maintained at the U.S. Department of Education website at http://studentaid. ed.gov. Click on the "Applying for Financial Aid" link to see a list of state higher education agencies. Once you find your state's agency, visit their website as well as contact them directly by phone.

Whether you are surfing their website or speaking to a representative, your goal is to learn about all of the opportunities available to you. While every state operates differently and not all have the same programs, here is an overview of the most common programs and resources that you should inquire about:

State Scholarships And Grants. Many states award their own state scholarships and grants. Make sure you understand how the scholarship works, who is eligible and if you need to apply by a certain deadline. Depending on your state there may be grants specifically for adults students, students who recently received their GED, vocational and technical school students and, of course, undergraduate and graduate school students. Some of these grants will be need-based while others will have no bearing on your financial situation. In some cases all you need to do is file an application to claim your money.

Private Scholarship List. As a clearinghouse for all things related to paying for college, many state agencies also maintain a list of private scholarships that are available. On some of the state websites we have found invaluable information including lists of all local civic groups that award scholarships.

State Loan Repayment Programs. Your state might sponsor valuable loan repayment programs depending on what you plan to study. Some states, for example, will help you pay back your student loan if you enter specific career areas such as teaching, law enforcement, medicine, nursing or technology. As long as you work within those fields in the state after graduation, the state will help you pay back your student loans.

State Work-Study. Like Federal Work-Study some states have their own work-study programs. These programs subsidize your salary as you work either on campus or for a government or nonprofit agency. Through work-study you can earn thousands of extra dollars while you go to school.

Tuition Exchange. Some states or state university systems have agreements with other states or specific universities in other states to let each other's residents attend at in-state or heavily discounted rates. Paying in-state rates at another state's school can save you thousands of dollars. Often these agreements are made with neighboring states.

Tuition Equalization Grants. These programs are designed to help shrink the difference in the cost of tuition between public and private universities. In Georgia, for example, residents who attend a more expensive private college can qualify to receive a tuition equalization grant of up to $1,045 per year.

Retraining Grants. Some state agencies also administer retraining programs for workers who have been laid off. These programs specifically target adults who intend to go back to school to learn a new trade or skill that will help them find employment. In Minnesota, for example, more than 1,300 laid off workers received training grants worth $4.3 million. The money was distributed through the Minnesota Jobs Skills Partnership Board. If you are going back to school to get a better job, you should inquire about retraining and displaced workers grants.

Disability Grants. Most states offer financial assistance to students who are disabled. The programs vary from state to state as do the qualifications for being classified as disabled. However, if you are disabled you should begin investigating this option early since it can take several months or even a year to get certified for the appropriate program.

Senior Citizen Discounts. If you're over 60 in some states you not only get discounts on dinner but you also get to take college courses at a significant discount or even for free! Check with both your state agency as well as your university to find out what kind of discounts are available to senior citizens.

Other Funding Resources And Services. Be sure to ask about all of the other resources and services that your state offers. Some sponsor workshops to help families apply for financial aid while others have their own publications that they will send you for free on how to pay for college.

It's important that you learn all that you can about the various programs offered by your state. Request all of the free information that they offer and take advantage of any resources such as lists of community scholarships that they provide.

Your College

Believe it or not but your college is your best ally when it comes to getting money. Sure they charge you for tuition but they can also give you financial aid, scholarships and grants. Colleges also receive money from alumni, community foundations and others to create scholarships for deserving students and staff various offices with knowledgeable administrators whose job is to help you figure out how to lower the sticker price of your education.

To make paying for college as painless as possible, take advantage of every opportunity and resource that your school offers. Following are the various services your college may offer to give you a road map for how to maximize their assistance.

Scholarships. Your college is one of the best places to find scholarships. Colleges give both need-based awards to students with low financial means as well as merit-based awards for everything from a student's interests to career goals. The challenge is that these scholarships are often spread throughout the university system. Many scholarships are administered by either the admission or financial aid office. Plus, your own department may also have specific awards for students in your major. To complicate things, various campus groups—such as the school newspaper—may also award scholarships to their members. Make sure you don't leave any stone unturned when looking for resources. As you search for scholarships on your campus be sure to check these places:

- Admission office
- Financial aid office
- Student development office
- Adult learning center

■ Career center

■ Library

■ Alumni clubs

■ Student clubs and organizations

■ Foundations

Transfer Scholarships. If you are transferring into a college from another school or community college you may qualify for a guaranteed transfer scholarship. If you are thinking about transferring, speak with the admission office at the colleges you are considering. Ask them what kind of financial aid package you may expect and inquire about transfer scholarships that you may be eligible to receive.

Tuition Reciprocity Agreements. Some schools have formed relationships with neighboring states to offer their residents automatic in-state rates from the beginning. The University of Arkansas, for example, offers a Non-Resident Tuition Award for entering freshmen from neighboring states that include Texas, Mississippi, Louisiana, Kansas, Missouri, Oklahoma and Tennessee. This may save you up to $6,000 a year in fees. If you want to attend a state college in a neighboring state, contact the admission office to find out if any such discount agreements are in effect.

Finally, you can always ask for more money from your college. Usually this means that you have submitted your financial aid application but the financial aid package that you receive from the college is just not enough to allow you to pay the tuition bills. If you can present a sound case for why the college's financial aid offer is not sufficient, you may be able to convince the college to give you more assistance.

Your Employer

There are many reasons why a company would want to help you pay for your education. The obvious reason is if your education helps you do a better job. By paying for a computer course, for example, your employer knows that you'll be able to use these newly-learned skills to improve your daily work and therefore become a more productive employee.

Another reason a company would be willing to pay for your education is that it is a benefit for recruiting better workers. If you are choosing between two similar jobs but one offers to pay for career development classes that you take while employed, you will probably accept their job offer.

The last reason why a company would offer to help you pay for your education is in order to keep you. Since you only get these benefits as an employee, you must continue to work for the company while you are also getting your schooling. Some companies may even make you sign an agreement to work for them for a certain number of years in order to receive education benefits. It's a trade. The company agrees to pay for your education, and you agree to work for them for a certain amount of time.

There is no standard education benefit, and companies are free to create whatever they feel is most useful to their employees as well as affordable for their bottom lines. In general, you will find that education benefits will fit into one of the following categories:

Tuition Assistance. The most common program that your employer will offer is tuition assistance or reimbursement. Companies are free to set their own policies on how these programs work. They may pay for a percentage of your tuition, up to a specific dollar amount or for a number of units. Most tuition assistance programs have a grade requirement, which means that if you earn lower than a "B" or "C," your company is not obligated to pay.

Companies usually pay only for courses that are deemed "work-related." Fortunately, "work-related" is a broad definition that is open for interpretation. You can often make a convincing case for courses that are not related directly to the job that you are doing now but that will help you develop professionally and learn new skills to advance in your career. Take a look at the people who are above you and see what skills and educational backgrounds they have. It makes perfect sense for you to take courses to learn those same skills so that you may be promoted to those positions in the future.

It's important that you talk to your human resources or personnel department and understand all of the rules to qualify for tuition assistance at your company. While many companies have tuition assistance, it is not always widely publicized. We've heard of more than one instance where an adult student spoke to their HR department only to be told they didn't have tuition assistance. Yet, when they asked their direct manager they found out that there was a program but it was run through their department manager and not HR. So be sure to inquire with both your HR department and your department manager.

Finally, be aware that some companies will withhold paying your benefits for up to a year to make sure that you stay at your job. If you quit within a certain period after completing your courses, they may deduct what they have paid from your last paycheck. So don't think about taking advantage of tuition assistance if you plan on jumping ship soon.

Tuition Discounts. Your company may have a deal with schools in your area for discounts on certain classes or programs. For example, you may be able to take a computer training class for free or at a steep discount. Or, if you work for a college or university (even if you are a part-time employee) you may receive significant discounts on courses. Many colleges even allow their employees to get a complete education for free.

Free Professional Development Classes. These classes are scheduled by your company and are usually held on site or at a local school. They often cover material that is directly related to your job function. For example, if you work in sales, you may be able to attend a training course on negotiation skills.

Many adults find that these free training classes are not in their company's written employee policy. However, when they inquire with their managers they learn that they can take up to several thousand dollars worth of training classes. Usually your department manager is allocated a set budget at the beginning of the year for employee education. Since this budget changes with the fortunes of the company, it is not something that can be guaranteed to every employee. Your manager usually has discretion over these funds and gives them on a first come, first served basis. Ask your manager what kind of training money is available—and be sure to have an idea of what classes you want to take if funds are available.

Employer Scholarships. Many companies offer scholarships with no strings attached simply because you are an employee. These are great scholarships to win since you are competing against so few other people. Often the only requirement is that you be an employee. Even if you work part-time, you may find that you are eligible to win an employee scholarship.

Federal And State Retraining Programs

From the federal government there are several programs that you can take advantage of, particularly if you have been laid off or downsized. On the state level you will find a much wider variety of resources that are open to more than recently displaced workers. Often the state will work with a network of charities, foundations, adult education centers and vocational and university systems to create a wide selection of services. Some of these services may be free while others are heavily discounted as long as you qualify for the program. Here are some places to start looking:

One Stop Career Center. These centers act as clearinghouses for information and programs offered by both the state and federal government. You can find a directory of all of the One Stop Career Centers at www.servicelocator.org. You may also call toll-free, (877) US-2JOBS.

Department Of Labor Adult Training Programs. Most adult training programs are authorized by the Workforce Investment Act. This federal program aims to increase occupational skills, improve the quality of the workforce, reduce welfare dependency and enhance the productivity and competitiveness of the nation's economy. Most services are provided through One Stop Career Centers and include both occupational training and training in basic skills. There are also support services including assistance with transportation and childcare to enable an individual to participate in the program.

Educational Opportunity Centers. There are 139 federally-funded Educational Opportunity Centers located throughout the country. These centers primarily serve displaced or underemployed workers from families with incomes under $24,000. Unfortunately, there is no national directory of EOCs. The best way to find them is to do an Internet search for "Educational Opportunity Center" along with the name of your state. Often these centers are based out of a college. Once you find an EOC in your state, contact them to find the EOC nearest you.

Tax Breaks

Instead of writing a check to the IRS, why not get a tax break from them? Give yourself up to $1,650 with the Hope tax credit. This tax credit reduces your taxes dollar for dollar and is like putting money directly into your pocket. You may receive up to $1,650 in Hope credits if you are in your first or second year of an undergraduate degree or certificate program. (Unfortunately, graduate and professional programs are excluded from this tax credit.) Once you are past your sophomore year, you cannot claim this credit. Also, repeating a year doesn't count.

To figure out how much of a Hope tax credit that you can claim, look at the total amount of money that you paid out of your own pocket for tuition. The Hope credit can only be used for tuition, not room and board and other expenses. Once you know how much you've paid out of pocket for tuition, you can claim 100 percent of the first $1,100 and 50 percent of the next $1,100 that you paid. In other words to claim the full $1,650 you must have paid at least $2,200 in qualified education expenses.

To claim a Hope tax credit, file your taxes using Form 1040 or 1040A and attach Form 8863 Education Credits. There are a few other stipulations attached to the Hope credit, which are that the you must be enrolled at least half-time, be enrolled in a program that leads to a degree, certificate or other recognized educational credential and be free of any felony conviction for possessing or distributing a controlled substance.

The other tax credit you may receive is up to $2,000 with the Lifetime Learning credit. The Lifetime Learning credit is similar to the Hope credit and reduces the tax you owe dollar for dollar. But unlike the Hope, the Lifetime Learning credit can be used for any year of college, graduate school or even continuing education. However, you cannot claim both a Hope and a Lifetime Learning credit in the same year. It is usually to your advantage to claim the Hope for the first two years and then the Lifetime Learning credit for the next two years.

If you have already completed your first two years of undergraduate work, are taking continuing education courses or are a graduate school student, then you have no choice but to take the Lifetime Learning credit.

The maximum amount of the Lifetime Learning credit is $2,000 per tax return, which is figured by taking 20 percent of what you pay for tuition (not room and board or other expenses) up to $10,000. This means that to claim the full $2,000 credit, you must spend $10,000 or more out of your own pocket on tuition. Remember, money that is already receiving a tax benefit like scholarships that are tax-free or 529 Savings Plan money doesn't count in figuring out how much you spent. The IRS doesn't allow double-dipping.

Eligible courses can be part of a postsecondary degree program or taken to acquire or improve job skills. Eligible educational institutions include any college, university, vocational school or other postsecondary educational institution eligible to participate in a student aid program administered by the Department of Education. This includes virtually all accredited, private or public, nonprofit and proprietary (privately owned, profit-making) postsecondary institutions. Also, the felony drug conviction rule that might prevent you from getting a Hope credit does not apply for the Lifetime Learning credit.

To claim either of these tax credits, you must also meet the income requirements. For a single taxpayer you can get the full credit if your modified adjusted gross income does not exceed $45,000. If it does but is below $55,000 you can claim a partial credit. For married couples filing jointly you can get the full credit if your income does not exceed $90,000. If you earn more but are still below $110,000 you can claim a partial credit.

Since you can claim only one of the credits per year, make sure you take advantage of them in the right order. If you qualify for both then you probably want to use the Hope credit in the first two years and then the Lifetime Learning credit in the years thereafter. The Hope credit lets you qualify for the full amount while using less of your own money.

Other Tax Deductions

Tax deductions are not as good as tax credits but they do reduce your taxable income, which means you will still pay less taxes. One of the most common education deductions is for money that you pay for tuition and fees. This can be the tuition that you paid for yourself, a spouse or a dependent child. You can deduct up to $4,000 of tuition expenses (not room and board or other expenses) that you paid as long as you are not also claiming a Hope or Lifetime Learning credit. This is part of the no double-dipping rule, which also means that you cannot deduct any tuition expenses that you paid with tax-free money such as funds from scholarships.

To claim the full deduction you must also meet income requirements. If you are a single taxpayer with a modified adjusted gross income of $65,000 or less or a couple filing jointly with an adjusted gross income of $130,000 or less you can take the full deduction. If you make more but still less than $80,000 as a single taxpayer or $160,000 as a joint taxpayer you can deduct only up to $2,000 in tuition expenses.

All student loan interest that you pay is tax deductible up to $2,500 per year. The loan must have been used for qualified higher-education expenses, including tuition, fees, room and board, supplies and other related expenses. Also the maximum allowable deduction is gradually reduced for single taxpayers whose modified adjusted gross income exceeds $50,000 but is below $65,000 and for married taxpayers filing jointly whose modified adjusted gross income exceeds $105,000 but is below $135,000.

You can usually count as interest the loan-origination fees (other than fees for services), capitalized interest, interest on revolving lines of credit and interest on refinanced student loans, which include both consolidated loans and collapsed loans. You can also count any voluntary interest payments that you make. To claim the deduction you should receive form 1098-E from your lender or loan servicer.

If you have a generous employer you might be able to receive up to $5,250 of tax-free employer provided educational assistance benefits each year. This means that you may not have to pay tax on amounts your employer pays for your education including payments for tuition, fees and similar expenses, books, supplies and equipment. This can be used for both undergraduate and graduate-level courses. Plus, the payments do not have to be for work-related courses. However, you cannot use any of the tax-free education expenses paid for by your employer as the basis for any other deduction or credit, including the Hope and Lifetime Learning credits.

Tax questions are never easy and it is essential that you talk to a professional accountant. In addition, tax laws are constantly changing. To get the latest (and free) information, surf over to the IRS website at www.irs.gov or schedule a phone or personal appointment. You can call with questions to (800) 829-1040, or try the IRS's Everyday Tax Solutions service by calling your local IRS office to set up an in-person appointment. If you have access to TTY/TDD equipment, call (800) 829-4059.

Personal Savings

College is an investment in your future. With few exceptions you are going to have to contribute some amount of your own money to pay for it. While it is always better to get free cash from scholarships and financial aid, the reality is that the more you save, the more options you'll have.

Your personal savings is your best ally when it comes to paying for college. Scholarships are still contests with no guarantees that you'll win. Financial aid changes each year depending on the budgets of the government and college. There is also no guarantee, even if you deserve it, that you will receive all of the financial aid that you need to pay for school.

Plus if you are like most students and need to take out a student loan, your savings will multiply in value. For example, let's say that you need to borrow $50,000 to pay for college. At 8 percent interest over 10 years (the typical term for a student loan) you would end up paying more than $22,700 in interest. But if you were able to save half of that amount and borrowed only $25,000, you would pay only $11,400 in interest. That means your personal savings just helped you to avoid $11,300 in additional interest payments. For each dollar that you save you not only need to borrow one less dollar but you also save on the interest that you would have to pay.

The bottom line is that your savings is your money. You have total freedom to use it at whichever college you want. Nothing is as flexible as your own money.

One way to supercharge your saving is to take advantage of Individual Development Accounts. IDAs are designed for low-income workers to quickly save money for school by matching their savings. The idea is that if you are low income and working, the best way for you to improve your status is to build your savings, which can then be used to purchase an asset such as a house, business or education. To help speed this process, the Individual Development Account was established and is managed by a network of non-profit organizations. If you qualify for the IDA program you will set up a goal such as saving $2,000 for college. When you reach that goal, the IDA network will match what you saved by a ratio of two, three or even seven times that amount. Matched funds come from financial institutions, foundations, religious congregations and state and local governments.

For example, if you receive a 2:1 match, which is the most common, each time you deposit $10, you will get an additional $20 credited to your goal. When you reach your goal, the money is released directly to the college to pay for your tuition. Having your savings matched speeds up the time it takes for you to reach your goal.

IDA programs usually set their own specific participation requirements. In general, you must be within 200 percent of poverty. This works out to less than $18,000 for an individual or $37,000 for a family of four. (Be sure to check with your participating IDA program since these levels do vary.) IDA participants must also be employed and agree to take financial planning classes sponsored by the nonprofit organization.

The hardest part of participating in an IDA program is finding them. Since the network of IDA providers is composed of a hodge-podge of agencies, there is no national directory. You will have to do some digging. Start with all of the foundations and nonprofits in your area. Also try contacting the manager at your local banks. Visit the IDA Network website (www.cfed.org) to find the contact information for various IDA programs in your state. This will give you an idea of what you are looking for.

Once you find one in your area, make sure you understand the participation guidelines. If you qualify, you can definitely speed your way to your educational goal.

Learning More

This chapter is just an introduction to the many ways that you can pay for college. After all, we wrote an entire book on the subject, *501 Ways for Adult Students to Pay for College*. It's important to remember that there are many ways to pay for college, and if you put your mind to it, you will find a way to make your college or graduate school affordable.

Balancing Your Studies And Your Life

Balancing Your Studies And Your Life

Being an adult student is like being a multitasking superhero. You may need to balance cramming for an exam, caring for a family, working part-time and, of course, sleep all in a single day. No one claims that this is easy to do. However, there are some steps that you can take to prevent yourself from going entirely crazy trying to do it all. If you think about your goals and commitments, map out your schedule and select the right kind of program before you start your studies, you will set yourself up to succeed.

Since you're about to embark on an exciting but challenging adventure, we would like to share with you the strategies that adult students have used before to successfully balance all of their responsibilities.

Work Your Schedule

Before you start your studies, you should take a hard look at your schedule and expectations. Consider the time that you need to spend with your family, work and other commitments that you have. This will help you figure out how much time you can dedicate to your studies and how quickly you can finish a program.

You may find that it will be better for you to study part-time, that you only have enough time to work part-time instead of full-time or that you need some extra help with childcare. It helps to map out a typical week for you, scheduling in your classes, work, study time and family and personal time.

Consider the schedule of your classes. Would it be better to attend a program part-time even though it may take longer to get your degree? Would daytime, weekend or evening classes fit you best? Do you need the very flexible hours of a distance-learning program?

It helps to review your options and select the right kind of program that can accommodate the other important things in your life. You may not get your degree as quickly as you would like, but this may help you succeed academically and balance life outside of your studies.

Get Your Family On Board

If you have a family, then you know that it sometimes takes an official treaty among all members to keep the peace. Because you will be adding the extra layer of your studies to the mix, you'll want to work with your family beforehand to set expectations. Have a family sit-down in which you explain why you are pursuing your education, how this will help your family in the long run and how this will impact them. Here are some things to discuss with your family:

Financial impact of your education and how the family budget may be affected by tuition bills. It will help for your family to understand why your education is worth the investment and which expenses may be cut.

Household chores and responsibilities. Will family members need to take more responsibility around the house? Organize who will do which chores.

Time that you can spend with your family. This may mean that you need additional help with childcare or that you will need to carve out time to spend with your family.

Study time. You may need to set ground rules for being left alone while you study. You may have to establish hours of the day when you cannot be disturbed unless it's an emergency or dedicate a specific room in your house as your place of study.

Benefits of your studies. Explain to your family why it is important for you to resume your studies and what your goals are for your education. Describe how your goals will help strengthen your family in the long-term.

Timeline. Share your timeline for getting your degree or finishing your program. Let your family know how long you will be in school and when you expect to finish. It helps to have your family cheering you on to the finish.

After having this discussion with your family, you may be surprised at the lengths to which they go to make your studies easier. They will understand why you want to further your education and provide the support that you need to succeed.

Become A Bookworm

A common recurring nightmare for many new adult students is sitting down to take an exam and suddenly realizing that you haven't studied. Perspiring and with racing heart you find yourself lost among the test questions, desperate and hopeless. It's no surprise that many adult students fear returning to school, cracking open the textbooks and taking midterms for the first time in many years.

The good news though is that for most adult students the fear is unfounded. You will learn to pick up where you left off, relearning your study skills. Many adult students find that they do better than traditional students because they are more focused on their goal of attaining a degree, have real-world experience to help them in their studies and have fewer distractions from the social side of college life.

Still, this doesn't mean that you will instantly become a super student. You can take steps to help make the transition from real world to academic easier:

Don't be afraid to ask questions. The truth is that for every question that you ask, there are five other students who want to ask the same question. The difference is that you have the confidence to ask questions. An important part of the educational process is the back and forth that happens between professor and students. You can learn as much from classroom discussions as you can from lectures.

Take advantage of office hours. If you have questions that you don't want to ask in front of the whole class, you want to discuss a topic in greater detail or you need help with a paper, drop by your professor's office hours. They will be more than happy to give you the personal attention that you need.

Get an extra boost if you need it. Besides your professor, the next best person to help you learn is a student who has successfully completed a class before you. You can easily find tutors for almost any subject at your school. At some schools, tutoring is provided at no or low-cost to adult students.

Take advantage of teamwork. You may learn well on your own, but you may learn even better in a study group. Form one to work on assignments together and to study for exams.

Know when your peak study times are. If you are a night owl, don't try to study when you first wake up. It's important that you figure out when your best times to study are and then stick to those times.

Set aside a time and place to study. With all that goes on in your life, it's important to dedicate enough time and the right place to study to set yourself up to succeed.

Take Advantage Of What Your School Offers

One of the reasons why tuition is so expensive is because it provides more to you than a seat in a lecture hall. All colleges and universities offer additional services, whether they are social, academic or cultural. To make the most of your education, make use of as many of these as possible. Here are some to consider:

Academic assistance. Most schools offer extra help for students through tutoring. Even if your school does not have a formal tutoring office, you can arrange for tutoring help on your own by posting notices in the department in which you need help. You may also find additional resources like lectures on tape at your school.

Lectures and debates. Colleges and universities are home to some of the most stimulating lectures and debates. You may be able to listen to prominent politicians, historians, artists and more through your school.

Career services office. Almost every school has a career services office. This is where you will find job listings and where recruiters will visit to interview students on campus. You may also be able to get help with resume writing and interview practice. Visit your career services office to find out what resources it offers.

Alumni office. Following the old saying that it's not what you know but who you know, visit your school's alumni office. This office usually keeps a database of alumni and their employment history. You may find someone at the company or in the field that you desire to work in, and it helps to introduce yourself as a student at their alma mater.

Adult student center. Some schools have lounges or centers for adult students. Here you can learn about the services for adult students as well as socialize with other students who are similar to you.

Clubs and organizations. Schools typically offer dozens of campus organizations, which means that you will most likely find one that appeals to your interests. If you have the time, get involved in one to pursue your interests as well as meet more students.

Recreation. Colleges and universities often have facilities that top the best health clubs, and as a student you should take advantage of them.

Museums. As a student, you may get free or reduced admission to your school's museums.

Arts. Colleges and universities are the host of some of the most economical entertainment to be found. Enjoy campus theatre, music and dance.

Childcare. Your school may provide economical options for childcare. At some schools, students who wish to go into early childhood education provide services at cut-rate prices.

Medical care. Because you are a student, you may want to take advantage of your school's medical insurance.

You are not alone. As you face the numerous challenges of going back to school, know that thousands of adults have gone before you and have successfully balanced school, work and family life. That doesn't mean that it was easy. Of course, that can be said of almost anything worthwhile in life.

Look at where you are now and where you'd like to be, and see how your education will help you get there. We think that if you keep your end goal in mind, you will find the motivation to open that textbook, negotiate the demands of student and family life and obtain the degree that you seek.

Parting Words

Going back to college is a major life decision. There will invariably be a few obstacles and challenges that lie ahead. However, the rewards are well worth the effort. Your education is one of the most important investments that you can make it yourself. It will improve your life—both professionally and personally.

Of the many hundreds of adults who we met while researching this book, we didn't meet a single one who regretted their decision to go back to school. These adults are proving that learning is a life-long adventure. Through their struggles and successes it is clear that there is nothing that can stop someone who is determined to reach their educational goals. As you embark on your own journey, we wish you the best!

About The Authors

Harvard graduates and husband and wife team Gen and Kelly Tanabe are the founders of SuperCollege and the award-winning authors of nine books including *501 Ways For Adult Students to Pay For College*, *Get Free Cash For College*, *1001 Ways to Pay For College*, *Get Into Any College* and *Accepted! 50 Successful College Admission Essays*.

Together, Gen and Kelly were accepted to every school to which they applied, including all of the Ivy League colleges, and won over $100,000 in merit-based scholarships. They were able to graduate from Harvard debt-free.

Gen and Kelly give workshops across the country and write the nationally syndicated "Ask The SuperCollege.com Experts" column. They have made hundreds of appearances on television and radio and have served as expert sources for *USA Today*, the *New York Times*, the *U.S. News & World Report*, the *Chronicle of Higher Education*, *CNN* and *Seventeen*.

Gen, Kelly, their son Zane and dog Sushi live in Belmont, California.